Business Continuity Management

An essential resource to navigate a fast-changing and challenging world, this book presents core concepts and practical insights for enterprise risk management, business continuity management, and organizational resilience.

Business continuity management is a critical aspect that investors and company directors evaluate in terms of an organization's sustainability and future value propositions in the face of supply chain disruptions, threats of economic recession, climate change, and the COVID-19 pandemic. This guide demonstrates a simple and systematic way to ensure that businesses are prepared for any crisis or emergency, including steps to meet the specific requirements prescribed in the international Business Continuity Standard ISO 22301, with a particular focus on the oil and gas sector. The seasoned author team brings their experience to bear on critical issues such as:

- Where managers lose focus on the need for business continuity – and how to regain it.
- How to select and implement a business continuity management tool.
- How to plan for the "macro scenario" that combines supply chain management, risk management, business continuity, and crisis management.
- How to best utilize "peace time" to explore business continuity plans and strategies.
- Why organizations should invest in business continuity even when the "going is tough in revenue and sales."

This guide to understanding the role of business continuity and management as an organizational strategy will earn its place on the desks of senior leaders, health and safety directors, consultants, corporate trainers, and business continuity and risk management professionals.

Kush Srivastava, MBCI, BCCE, ISO 22301 Lead Auditor, CRM, CIF, is a global award-winning seasoned Business Continuity, Crisis and Risk

Management practitioner and consultant who was inducted into the BCI Hall of Fame in 2019 by The Business Continuity Institute, UK. He has 30+ years of experience in assessing, designing, and customizing BCMS frameworks leading to organizations being resilient and crisis ready across the management hierarchy. He is a contributor to the framing of UAE's Business Continuity Management Standard, NCEMA7000.

Dr Waddah S. Ghanem Al Hashmi, BEng (Hons), MBA, MSc, AFIChemE, FEI, FIEMA, MIoD, FBDIGCC, FIIRSM, is a certified director and respected industry specialist. He is an authority with a passion for improving the QHSE and the overall success of compliance, governance, and leadership systems in the energy sector. He has a distinguished career as a leader and functional director who demonstrates in-depth knowledge of all facets of technical, operational, and procedural systems. He has international education and compliance experience in Asia, Europe, North Africa, and the Middle East. He is a published author with strong postgraduate engineering, sciences, and management education and is fluent in both English and Arabic.

Business Continuity Management

Significant Insights from Practice

**Kush Srivastava and
Dr Waddah S. Ghanem Al Hashmi**

 Routledge
Taylor & Francis Group

NEW YORK AND LONDON

Designed cover image: © Getty

First published 2024
by Routledge
605 Third Avenue, New York, NY 10158

and by Routledge
4 Park Square, Milton Park, Abingdon, Oxon, OX14 4RN

Routledge is an imprint of the Taylor & Francis Group, an informa business

© 2024 Kush Srivastava and Dr Waddah S. Ghanem Al Hashmi

Library of Congress Cataloguing-in-Publication Data
Names: Srivastava, Kush, author.
Title: Business continuity management : significant insights from practice / Kush Srivastava and Dr Waddah S. Ghanem Al Hashmi.
Description: New York : Routledge, 2024. | Includes bibliographical references and index.
Identifiers: LCCN 2023023809 (print) | LCCN 2023023810 (ebook) | ISBN 9781032303567 (hbk) | ISBN 9781032303512 (pbk) | ISBN 9781003304678 (ebk)
Subjects: LCSH: Industrial management. | Success in business.
Classification: LCC HD31.2 .S655 2024 (print) | LCC HD31.2 (ebook) | DDC 658--dc23/eng/20230720
LC record available at https://lccn.loc.gov/2023023809
LC ebook record available at https://lccn.loc.gov/2023023810

ISBN: 978-1-032-30356-7 (hbk)
ISBN: 978-1-032-30351-2 (pbk)
ISBN: 978-1-003-30467-8 (ebk)

DOI: 10.4324/9781003304678

Typeset in Optima
by MPS Limited, Dehradun

Contents

Foreword

I am fortunate to have known Kush Srivastava for over a decade now and have always been impressed by his passion for thinking out of the box on issues and matters relating to business continuity and its related domains. His ability to apply pragmatically business continuity matters in an organizational context is, I feel, a key strength.

In this publication, Kush, as a thinking professional, endeavors to leverage his vast experience of over 30 years in different sectors and industries covering banking, financial services, insurance, IT (Information Technology) and IT-enabled services, business process outsourcing, shared services, and the oil, gas, and energy sectors. His approach and insights are based on his hands-on practical operational experience utilizing the organizational resources most optimally while keeping a keen eye on the constraints and organization culture. His keen sense of understanding of the people, process, and technology aspects is reflected in this publication as he draws a clear path for management teams and business continuity management (BCM) practitioners and managers to follow in preparing organizations for their resilience journey. This is expressly covered in various chapters of his book, where he renders his experiential wisdom for executive leaders and company boards in their journey to seek organizational resilience.

In topical chapters, the length and breadth of the topics are covered while addressing critical factors and aspects that can create resilient and stable organizations, preventing them from becoming the very cause of their peril! The chapter on the aspect of automation of business continuity demonstrates acumen of complete understanding of business continuity as a science, art, and practice and offers deep insight for senior management to consider organization maturity and readiness before putting the valuable investments towards a BCM tool purchase. The book has proficiently covered the critical milestones that senior management and top executives must endeavor and aspire for during what is referred to as peace time and business as usual, including a list of best practices – which help prepare organization's capability to withstand any crisis, emergency, or outage.

There are some truly relevant diktats that are suggested that will stand in good stead for companies to deal with any crisis or emergency. These tips also cover the downside in organization performance when it is incurring losses or earning less than their potential. Some of the solutions suggested by him are extremely relevant in today's ever-changing corporate dynamics and economic environment. I have greatly enjoyed such insights and guidance. While I can go on and on, on the value and benefits of the contents of this book, I will emphasize that the effort that has clearly been invested in this publication will greatly help BCM practitioners, managers, and crisis, as well as ITDR (Information Technology Disaster Recovery) professionals, in improvising their skills and acumen for dealing and resolving a difficult situation arising from crisis, emergency, or disruption. The author's clear ability to comprehend the 360-degree aspect during crucial times and guidance towards a well-considered solution based on matured thinking and analysis can be of immense value to BCM practitioners and personnel.

I can say that Kush Srivastava, with the great editing efforts of Dr. Waddah Ghanem Al Hashmi, has created a great source of information and guidance in the domains of business continuity, crisis, and risk management. It also is a useful resource to use to aid effective IT Disaster Recovery planning. This book will also help practitioners in these domains in understanding the macro-aspects of BCM on organizational economics and its significance for the future existence of organizations while successfully achieving their vision and mission.

Margaret J. Millett

MsBC, FBCI (Hon), MBCP

Head of Global Resilience at Uber, USA.

Global Resilience Leader | International Speaker |

Award Winner

Abbreviations

Abbreviation	Definition
BCM	Business Continuity Management
AHS	Airport Hydrant System
BC DRP	Business Continuity Disaster Recovery Plan
BCMS	Business Continuity Management Systems
BIA	Business Impact Analysis
BOD	Board of Directors
CEO/CXO	Chief Executive Officer
COO	Chief Operations Officer
CTO	Chief Technology Officer
CMP	Crisis Management Plan
CySec	Cyber Security
ERP	Emergency Response Plan
IMP	Incident Management Plan
IMT	Incident Management Team
IT DR	Information Technology - Disaster Recovery
IT DRP	IT Disaster Recovery Plan
ITS	Information Technology System
MAO	Maximum Acceptable Outage
MBCO	Minimum Business Continuity Objective
MRP	Media Response Plan
MTPOD	Maximum Tolerable Period od Disruption
O&G	Oil and Gas
O, G & E	Oil, Gas and Energy
OTP	Original Tool Provider
OTS	Operations Technology System
RA	Risk Assessment
RPO	Recovery Point Objective
RTO	Recovery Time Objective

SCRM	Supply Chain Risk Management
SLA	Service Level Agreement
SOP	Standard Operating Procedures
SPOF	Single Point of Failure

About the Authors

Principle Author
Mr Kush Srivastava
MBCI, BCCE, ISO 22301 Lead Auditor, DCML, CRM, CIF, MCOM, M.GCCBDI

Kush is an award-winning, certified BCM Professional with 18+ years of experience leading and delivering global resilience engagements across multiple industries and domains such as Utilities, Oil & Gas, Banking, Financial Services, BPO, ITES, Crisis Management and BCP-DR consulting.

He has the ability to assess, design, and implement business resilience & crisis readiness with due alignment & comprehensiveness of Incident Management Plans, Emergency Response Plans, Crisis Management Plans, Business Continuity Plans, and Crisis Media Resp. Plans of complex organizations. He is a regular invitee/speaker/panelist at various international BCM Conferences and Summits.

He has the distinction of being one of the BCM Professionals in UAE to be recognized and awarded by NCEMA (UAE BCM Regulator) for his contribution in developing the UAE BCM Standard & Guidelines (AE/SCNS/ NCEMA 7001:2015). He has extensive project and hands-on operational expertise in *"simplifying the governance model and BCMS documentation for complex/multi layered organizations."* He has the distinction of helping Boards and senior management for successful implementation of BCM program and organization deriving value for all its stakeholders.

His quick grasp of *"nuts and bolts in the organization"* helps him in assessing and bridging the gap from *"as is situation"* and organization's wish list of *"being crisis ready across all hierarchical levels."* He has helped management in devising customized tests and exercises that prepare organizations' people, process, and technology for their "rainy day actions" while also addressing organizations' pain points."

He is an MBCI of The BCI, UK, and is a double-certified ISO 22301 Lead Auditor from ICOR USA and ISC Australia. He is a certified Business Continuity Expert from BCMI Singapore. He also holds Certificate in International Finance from IIT-Delhi, India. He holds a master's degree in Commerce from Delhi University and Diploma in Corporate and Management Laws from Indian Law Institute, New Delhi.

He won the Continuity and Resilience Professional Award in 2018 & 2019 at the BCI Middle East Awards and the Global Award for Continuity and Resilience Professional Award 2019 at the BCI Global Awards 2019. He has been inducted into the BCI Hall of Fame in 2019.

He lives in Dubai with his family of homemaker wife and daughter, pursuing a degree in computer application.

Chief Editor
Dr. Waddah S. Ghanem Al Hashmi
BEng (Hons), MBA, MSc, DBA, DipSM, DipEM, AFIChemE, FEI, FIEMA, MIoD, FBDIGCC, FIIRSM
    Fellow & UAE Chapter Advisory Chair, Board Directors Institute – GCC
    Hon. Chairman – Energy Institute – Middle East
    Chairman of the Federal Committee for Occupational Safety and Health
Sr Director at Emirates National Oil Company

Dr. Waddah S. Ghanem Al Hashmi is a Certified Director and a highly respected industry specialist and authority with a passion for improving the quality, environment, health, safety, and overall success of compliance, governance, and leadership systems in the energy sector. He has a distinguished career as a Chief Compliance Officer and Functional Director, demonstrating in-depth knowledge of all facets of technical, operational, and procedural systems with proven success in managing projects, developing functions from first principles, and building relationships that deliver significant, tangible results. He has international education and compliance experience in Asia, Europe, North Africa, and the Middle East. He has a strong postgraduate engineering, sciences, and management education and is fluent in both English and Arabic.

He is a UAE national with strong leadership and management acumen based on solid business, vocational, and academic foundations. He has good, diversified board experience. He is an effective lateral thinker with a passion for dealing with compliance and corporate governance issues, especially in both organizational and public domains. Diversely qualified in both technical and management fields, he has held several senior positions for the last 16 years, shaping the policies and principles for environmental, health, safety, and quality for the largest diversified Oil and Gas Company in Dubai, operating in the UAE, Singapore, South Korea, KSA, Djibouti, and Morocco. He is a passionate academic industrialist with a great interest in bridging the gap between vocational, academic, and experiential knowledge.

He has a strong and passionate approach to systems building and is a developer of startup and new projects. He has led a diversified portfolio of functions, including business excellence, legal affairs, corporate communications, EHS assurance, security, and enterprise risk management, as well as sustainability. He has assisted many different organizations on matters of EHS, Risk Management, and Sustainability (in both an office bearing and personal capacity) including Dubai International Airports, Dubai Police, Dubai Supreme Council of Energy (DSCE), ADNOC, and the Regional Clean Seas Organization (RECSO) as well as others.

He is affiliated with and has participated in various thought leadership activities with the GCC Board Directors Institute (BDI-GCC), Institute of Directors (IOD) India, and is a member of the IoD in the United Kingdom. He is also currently the Chairman of the Board of the Energy Institute Middle East and served as a council member of the Energy Institute in the UK for a three-year term elected from the International Chapters. He was the Vice Chairman of the Board of Dubai Carbon Centre of Excellence (DCCE PJSC) in which he chaired the NRC Committee. He is also the Vice Chairman of the Oil Companies International Marine Forum (OCIMF), which is the voice for the Oil and Gas Industry at the IMO. He is the Senior Advisor to the Board of the Clean Energy Business Council, UAE.

He has authored/published and co-authored eight internationally published books in addition to many practitioner-based technical conference articles and presentations. His publications include books in Safety Management, Operational Excellence, Reflective Learning, Governance and Leadership, and several other specialist areas. He has also published jointly and edited 2020 an article with the *Harvard Business Review Arabia* on the Connected Leadership Framework and in 2022 on Directorship. He also currently mentors board directors and is Chapter Chair for the UAE for the Board Directors Institute – GCC. He was born and is based in Dubai, United Arab Emirates.

Purpose of The Book

In a fast-changing world where several major challenges are facing organizations and forcing them to rethink their strategy, resilience, reliability and business continuity dimensions; this book provides a foundational guide to senior practitioners and seasoned leaders who are at the helm. The longevity and sustained existence of organisations is difficult to imagine in an ever more complex world and business environments without a sound understanding of reliability and effective business continuity management systems. The right understanding coupled with the right and timely decision in unfortunate situations of outage and emergency can be the differentiator for a resilient organization or its contra.

This book offers many important aspects that relate to business continuity from a very practical approach. Whilst it must be appreciated that there is an important role of business continuity management frameworks and standards, the imperatives that drive the effective practical implementation of solutions on issues resides very much in experiential knowledge and practice.

Through bringing together the thinking from the many standards in management systems and research from practice this book provides insights in to why many organisations and their leadership fails to effectively implement business continuity management. So, was it that the systems were built wrong, or ineffective to start with or was it that the implementation was ineffective for many organisations who clearly struggled to manage their business during the economic crisis and pandemic? Yet many organization leaders realized the lacunae due to certain misconceptions about their crisis readiness and the position of being a "Tiger turning out to be a Paper Tiger".

In this book the business continuity management (BCM) thinking and agenda by addressing an approach of the authors leveraging on experience with standards and with implementation and oversight of BCM. Essentially this practical book, is a guide for seasoned leaders and practitioners who have a good grounding in the fundamentals in business continuity and who have the experience and maturity to understand and appreciate some of the advanced concepts in this practice which is becoming so significant in the sustainability of organisations across all industry sectors.

The cross-industry experience with people, process and technology is essential to understand effectively in order to manage business continuity from the very perspective of resilience in depth. Even with technology, we must understand and appreciate that a maturity and sufficient inter-connectedness of the technology landscape is critical for the technology to drive the resilience in an organisation. For example, the book addresses how to move from manual to automatic modes, and when organisations can start to apply and implement BCM tools that will give management better assurance in implementation, effective maintenance, thought through scenario planning, and testing and exercising etc.

Culture change and organisational readiness is fundamental to success in terms of linking the people of the organisation with its systems and plans. In that sense the book talks about the key considerations for readying the organisation for the implementation of BCM. It delves into the aspect of culture and its correlation with a structured communication mechanism to aid effective and timely decision by the leaders of the organisation. Communication of the right data, at the correct detail in a timely manner must be underpinned by the clarity of the roles and responsibilities of every single function and person within the organisation. The book, as such addresses the main challenges that organisations face with respect to having legacy organisation structures that have failed to evolve towards dealing with crisis management, business continuity and resilience. The articles in the book will provide pointers and strong innuendoes to leaders of what must change in the legacies of the organization that will lead to changed and enhanced organizational resilience.

The ability to respond in a timely and effective manner when it comes to business continuity decision-making and the ability for the organisation to invoke or get ready to invoke the business continuity plans in the context of crisis management is discussed in some depth. The lack of a timely decision or a delayed decision could have long term impacts and the authors provide insight into some key indicators that will aid the CEO and senior managements in organizations.

In every industry sector today including energy, transport and logistics, manufacturing, medical and pharmaceutical, IT and technology, retail and generally supply chain businesses etc; the impact of evolving regulations; changing standards; and most importantly expectations and increased activism from stakeholders including customers, shareholders and even the regulators are driving significant changes in the expectations on business continuity management, resilience, and sustainability. The emerging risks due to ever-advancing technology puts across newer and more deadly risks and threats that can cripple 'organization if not dealt with in timely manner, apart from the fact that organizations now need to 'foresee, predict, and prepare against these UNKNOWNS'.

Thus, it is imperative that the ability of organisations to learn from global events, case studies and good practices is developed. The impacts that exist and the ones that have been seen across the evermore connected global trade and international businesses must form the knowledge in which continual improvement resides in the heart of the management systems thinking. This book is fundamentally based on pillars of high reliability organisational theory but is in essence a collection of sections or articles that address all the above.

We are confident that this book in its 10 short but concise chapters would provide seasoned leaders and BCM practitioners with the right level of foundational understanding required to implement effective business continuity management with good agility and sound holistic practical knowledge. They will be able to corelate the meaning, essence, preparedness, and response to any incident-emergency-crisis-business continuity requirement and pressing the "red button" for technological assistance in times of crisis or emergency.

Chapter 1

Where Do Leaders Falter in Implementing Business Continuity?

It would seem quite normal that leaders and senior managers in organizations across the corporate spectrum have their plate full in terms of daily, weekly, and monthly work schedules, so much so that at times these individuals are *so work over-loaded* that they compromise the organization's interest due to their lack of action, delayed actions, or inadequate attention due to the time constraints and adequacy of the time required for finding a solution for the issue at hand. Such instances are more common as we move up the hierarchy chain in any organization. The primary objectives – normally included in the company website as its mission and vision – get their fair share of importance while the related values pertaining to employee and stakeholder interest and safety get relegated to the following status: *we will deal with them if and when matters get worse or when the situation threatens financial viability, financial returns, or the company's reputation or it impacts our customers directly.*

Forward-looking CEOs, board directors, and senior leaders and managers have an approach of proactively planning for such contingencies and have specific strategies and plans to come out successful from such situation(s). These leaders practice pre-planning while visualizing "what could go wrong and how to deal with the situation." They anticipate the effect and impact of the risk and threat and its overall impact on the organization in the short, medium, or long term. This planning helps the organization to add confidence at the individual employee level and strengthen organization resilience.

History has shown us that organizations that have practiced pre-planning for business continuity have been able to come out more successful post crisis and emergency than those organizations that were ill-prepared. One important factor for this successful recovery is whether the leaders of such organizations make the right and timely investments (and provide adequate resources) in the implementation of business continuity across the organization. They provide for financial support,

DOI: 10.4324/9781003304678-1

resourcing, and operationalizing of business continuity governance and implementation. Some of the examples from history:

Example 1: Dominos Pizza "Obscene Video"
Year/Place: 2009/North Carolina, USA.
Incident: Posting of a "Food tainting video on YouTube by two employees as a prank."
The video went viral, damaging the company's image, and the company was trolled across the United States.

Company Response:

- Apology by Patrick Doyle, President of Dominos USA, stating the facts of the case and that the acts of 2 irresponsible employees do not represent the efforts of 25,000 employees of Dominos and 125,000 people associated with its supply chain across 60 countries.
- Action of firing the erring employees and review of hiring procedures.
- Emphasis on cleanliness and quality and customer trust as a key factor.

Enablers: Quick Decision/Damage Control/Root Cause Analysis (RCA)/ Corrective Action – Product Improvement – "Oven to Doorstep Tracking"
Result: 2011 Domino's Pizza named "Pizza Chain of the Year" in the USA

Example 2: United Airlines "Passenger Offload"/"Mishandled Customer Service"
Year/Place: Sunday 09th April 2017/Chicago O'Hare International Airport, USA.
Incident: Offloading of a passenger on an overbooked Flight 3411 (Scheduled dep 1640 hrs) from Chicago to Louisville.
Passenger Dr. David Dao, 69 (Vietnamese origin), refused US$1,000 coupon offer to leave the aircraft. He was one of the four passengers selected randomly by a computer.
Four United staff needed to operate a flight the next day from Louisville. The passenger was dragged out by security using brute physical force resulting in passenger having a broken nose bridge, two missing teeth, and concussions on his body.
Root Cause: Due to a technical snag on a flight at 2:55 pm earlier that day to Louisville, the four staff were reassigned to Flight 3411.

Company Response and Reactions:
Monday 10th Apr 2017 – Chairman Oscar Munoz wrote an internal email to employees appreciating the staff action and called the customer as "disruptive & belligerent."

Co-passengers trolled United and stated, "he was very polite as a matter of fact." United's 20% share on the United States–China route took a beating, with a customer base of 480 million users.

Customers posted videos of themselves cutting United Credit and Loyalty Cards.

Tuesday 11th Apr 2017 – "United market capital lost USD 1 Bn and 4% in value in 1 day against a cost of 4 seats." On 14th Apr 2017, Munoz apologized on national news, stating, *"truly horrific incident, understanding the outrage, anger & disappointment,"* while owning full responsibility. He accepted "Frontline staff not provided with tools, procedures, training and using common sense."

Enablers: Customer Apathy – Lack of Crisis Communication Procedures – Delayed Apology – Damage Done – Power of Social Media – Inadequate Facts before Public Statement (damage due to inappropriate words so "What I meant was …")

Result: Major Reputation Loss – Customer Attrition – Advantage to Competitors

From the cited cases, one can observe that in an organization similar to the ones above, the leaders and managers miss out on making the right decisions and taking the right steps for timely implementation of business continuity and crisis management. This results in the organizations, though having plans and strategies for dealing with crisis and outages, failing to protect the organization's interests as a result of such outages, irrespective of the duration. Some of the factors responsible for this "management oversight" are listed here:

• Governance: Unmonitored/Ill-Monitored

The organization's executive leadership and the Board of Directors must ensure that the organization embarks on its business continuity and resiliency journey in a timely manner and sets the due framework for implementing it across the organization. Leadership teams thus take adequate measures to put in place people and processes to accomplish the right outcome from these endeavors. They ensure that the relevant documentation to "run the program" exists in easy and understandable formats. The people know their roles and responsibilities. However, the battle is lost when all these provisions lack management oversight and a formal regular review process. In the medium and long term, these requirements become a *"form-filling exercise,"* and the organization's interests get compromised during and after any emergency or crisis. There is no proper and regular monitoring and a review process to establish *"how effective or relevant is the Business Continuity Management System (BCMS) program?"*

The management team of an organization establishes the "blueprint" for a successful and efficient BCMS with due clarity on roles and responsibilities, providing for finances, making arrangements for due resources, their training and awareness, etc., yet the part related to its proper implementation and governance is impacted by absence of action or delay in action.

• Culture as an Impediment

Every organization embodies a particular way and pattern of how its people act and conduct themselves in an ordinary course of business. One important outcome of an organization's culture is the allegiance of its employees and, consequently, their contribution to the organization's purpose. The motivation or the lack of it effects the level of their productivity, which will ultimately impact the bottom line and organization profitability. Culture also determines the longevity of employees' association with the organization, which in turn impacts the delivery and accomplishment of an organizational purpose of team pursuits. A disjointed team has its ills of a toxic work atmosphere with demotivated employees and staff using the organization as a steppingstone to serve their servile personal purpose.

Senior management and leaders should inculcate strong values and culture in the organization by practicing and setting examples. The values and culture need to be practiced daily and not as a one-off act. In the implementation of the BCMS, one of the most fundamental predictors of success is the discipline the organizational culture has in preparing the plans, practicing, and drilling them to assess their effectiveness and implementing the overall program.

• Weak Proliferation of Business Continuity Management

Normally a weak proliferation of Business Continuity Management (BCM) is reflective of the lack of adequate trust in implementing BCM by the senior management in the organization. This may be due to various reasons. Some of these are, but are not limited to:

- Nonalignment of the BCMS with the organization's priorities.
- Inability to make an investment in the BCMS for whatever reason.
- Vested interest of some stakeholders.
- Inability of management to convince the Board or Investors of the value of the BCMS.
- Organizational culture.

- "Orthodox thinking" of the organization as an entity. Orthodox thinking refers to a fatalistic thought process that disregards the possibilities of innovations and technological developments for a modern solution to traditional problems.

It is important for senior management to see the larger picture and its value for deciding in favor of implementing a BCMS. The value derived from its implementation and the confidence it gives to its stakeholders is a testimony that CEOs, CXOs, and the board members of organization decide in its favor while addressing the need to mitigate the ever-changing risk landscape.

Organizations must "prepare for the uncertain" as man-made and natural threats multiply. Management must constantly monitor the risk landscape and establish ways to detect risk profile changes quickly on a timely basis and effectively. Any lapse in this regard can have dire consequences for the company and its employees, even threatening its existence.

An organization needs a formal governance framework and relevant documentation to monitor risks and threats. Professionals with technical knowledge of crisis, emergency, business continuity, IT disaster recovery (DR), and other risks must implement them, and staff must be informed of this program's details and trained if necessary to ensure human safety and welfare. Management reviews and anomaly correction should be a formal process.

- **Budgets**

It has been observed and experienced many a time that an organization may have the clarity of implementing an effective business continuity program, yet due to one constraint or another, the organization is unable to achieve its objective. One of the prime reasons for this outcome is the lack of a proper budget or its inadequacy. Business continuity is an emerging domain, and management's are still grappling with certain aspects, such as:

- Who owns BCM?
- What resources are required for its effectiveness?
- What skills and experience are required for its implementation?
- Should the organization deploy an automated tool to expedite realizing the outcome?
- How should the cost of business continuity teams and its overheads be dealt with – financially?
- How should an organization view the costs associated with business continuity? Should it be owned by business units deriving value from it

or by the management as a company asset? Should it be considered a capital expenditure item or a revenue item while accounting for it in the financial books of the company? Should it be considered as an expense/liability in the company's balance sheet or as an investment/asset?

The International Business Continuity Standard, ISO 22301, requires organizations to have a predetermined number duly approved by the top/senior management as an approved budget for the organization's Business Continuity Program. It is up to the organization and at its discretion to allocate the budget among resource cost, its training and awareness, BCM automation tools, or any other "head" in this domain.

- **Weak/Inexperienced Business Continuity Managers**

It is a known fact that "Weak leadership can wreck the soundest of strategies." A weak manager often reflects:

- An unsure person.
- A person lacking skills and experience required to do a job.
- A person who fails to inspire his/her team.
- A person who is ineffective in a crisis or emergency.
- A person who may demotivate staff and the team during a crisis or emergency.

Due to rising risks and threats, organization resilience has become increasingly important. To continuously track the risk horizon, the organization must have the right technical or manual measures and procedures. In a crisis, a weak or inexperienced Business Continuity Manager will be viewed with suspicion and questioned about their ability to serve the organization. "A wrong person is manning the critical position of the BC Manager" may surprise businesses and other stakeholders with the management's choice of such a wrong person who is incapable of handling a crisis and emergency and other managers will be forced to face the consequences of such incompetence.

A Business Continuity Manager must lead crisis management and protect the company and its employees. He/she is the liaison between the Incident Management/Emergency Response team and top management for critical decisions affecting reputation, employee and customer interests, and company finances. With management approval, he/she must comply with regulations. In a crisis, Business Continuity Managers affect the recovery and continuity of critical operations and resource use. This sometimes shields the company from media, customers, and regulators. A well-prepared business continuity strategy and its related communication plan will determine how soon the company will resume its critical operations.

Forward looking and progressive organizations, while caring for their personnel, will also care for their "weak and inexperienced managers" as well. HR of such organizations normally deploy one or more of the following techniques:

- Identify the area of incompetence and develop a time bound plans to achieve desired results.
- Provide help to such managers using internal or external inputs.
- Confront/Challenge the manager in their weak domains to come out successful during a crisis or disruption.

The organization must ensure that after a period, the organization's business continuity readiness through its trained and experienced resources will meet this requirement.

• Skilled – Experienced Resources

The International Standard for Business Continuity requires organizations to deploy personnel who have an understating of the business continuity domain. They are expected to be experienced resources to manage the aspects of the business continuity framework, its structure, and requirements for implementation, and maintain the organization's BCMS. The Standard prescribes an implicit role and responsibility of leadership in implementing and maintaining an effective BCMS. The responsibility of ensuring that the outcome of the BCM program is in line with organizational pursuits is with top management or the senior leaders in the company.

HR should maintain records of training and experience in business continuity across the enterprise. It must facilitate refresher training on a periodic basis and should have a documented procedure for identifying Training Need Analysis (TNA). The organization's internal auditors also need to ensure the effectiveness of the BCM program and ensure that all requirements and provisions of the BCMS Standard are complied with.

• Over-Worked Staff

Every successful organization reflects the commitment and contribution of its staff in contributing to organizational pursuits. Such employees need to be adequately motivated to give their best performance, day after day. Organizations must remain relevant in the market and the morale and energy of its personnel should be channelized productively.

When workers and staff are being over-burdened by their day-to-day work pressures, they will have little time to think in a holistic manner regarding some of the basic norms that need to be followed in case of emergency or sudden outage. With respect to war times and crisis situations – it is the "peace time" initiatives that come in handy to assist the employees in doing things and following practices that will ensure the organization remains resilient. It is important to note that the plans and procedures for business continuity and managing crises are tested for their adequacy in such difficult times. BCM plans and the Crisis Management Plan should be carefully formulated, planned, tested, and reviewed, well in advance, prior to any crisis, emergency, or outage. It is thus of critical importance that the organization's personnel and management accomplish these initiatives in a holistic manner without any pressure.

As BCM is an emerging field, its readiness has been addressed differently by different organizations. A practice in one organization may not be suitable for the other or may need to be customized for the other organization, but what needs to be noted here is that the fundamental principles of effective business continuity, crisis management, IT DR, incident management, emergency response, and media response planning are similar, and all these should work in synchronization across all parts of the organization to achieve this. Its personnel should have the experience, time, willingness, and purposeful objectivity to achieve this at the entity level.

- **Complex Documentation**

In a crisis, organization staff should follow simple instructions. In a crisis or emergency, staff should follow pre-planned actions that benefit the organization. Given the same situation, different people may act differently, and staff must follow the process to avoid "hurting the interest" of the organization or its reputation. This mostly occurs due to staff's inherent nature as "risk takers" or "risk avoiders" or their understanding of risk as per their backgrounds, education, upbringing, and social environments. This is one of the main reasons management insists that crisis and emergency policies, procedures, and processes be written in simple, easy-to-follow language with adequate training. The employee must understand and follow the policy, procedure, and process requirement.

The authors have found that complex and complicated language in compliance documentation, such as policies, procedures, and process notes, can lead to confusion and compromise the organization's interests. This could hurt brand value, market share, organizational reputation, customer confidence, and stakeholder interests.

- **Untrained Business Continuity Champions**

A successful and progressive organization always believes in continuous training and learning until you get it right, and knowing alone is not enough; its knowledge must be applied practically. Willingness is not enough; it must be done practically. The essence of these statements is primarily to impress on the organization's need for trained, skilled, experienced, and competent resources to work towards organization's goals and vision. It is important for organization's management leaders to realize that to fly an airplane, you need a pilot, and for performing a heart surgery, you need a heart surgeon. Under normal circumstances, you cannot replace the pilot with a flight purser or air hostess, and you cannot replace a surgeon with a compounder or a nurse. This is because these jobs require services that are specific in nature, require high skill, and should not be performed by unskilled or untrained personnel.

As in the illustration above, the function of business continuity in any organization should be performed by a person with due knowledge, experience, and qualification in this domain. He/she may acquire this over time, but it is pertinent that they acquire the knowledge of the technical nuances over a definite period. With skills and experience acquired over time, such personnel are in a better position to understand and protect the interest of the organization while implementing business continuity effectively. They will ensure they understand the critical part of organization's key business operations, its drivers, its enablers, and its dependencies. Such trained BCM personnel can then contribute to enhancing the organization's resilience, and the organization can be better prepared to deal with an emergency, outage, or disruption.

- **Form-Filling Exercise**

Form filling is generally related to the aspect of the organization dealing with rules, regulations, policies, procedures, and guidelines required in its entirety or partially. This results in the organization having documented processes and procedures for most of the contingencies existing on paper only. In an organization, if the people, processes, and technology are not in sync with the regulatory requirements and regulatory compliance, this could lead to complications during and after an incident. Such organizations, when facing a crisis or emergency, fall short of protecting the organization's interest, its reputation, its market share, and its stakeholders, irrespective of their genre, be they employees, leaders, vendors, suppliers, service providers, counselors, auditors, or regulators.

Conclusion

As organizations move forward in their journey of resilience, their leaders and senior management must envision taking adequate management safeguards by timely embarking on the business continuity journey. Managements that do not practice this proactive approach for tomorrow's crisis, generally are plagued with a fake sense of confidence that can be dangerous for the organization in case of a crisis, outage, or emergency.

Such organizations that do not practice the tenets of safe business continuity could be in for a rude awakening, wherein inherently the *"Culture of Paper Tiger"* thrives across the organization and its personnel have a varied sense of responsibility.

Key Take-Aways

- For an organization to get the desired outcome from an incident or event, it should at least consider the impact of the incident or event on the organization's operations as well as its employees, customers, and stakeholders.
- Investment is required in BCMS as an imperative, as "there is no free lunch in life."
- Comprehensive congruence of an organizational initiative towards developing BCMS is a key driver for organization resilience.
- Keep reinventing the risk posture at regular intervals.
- Practicality of BCMS governance and its implementation should be simple and easy to implement.

Chapter 2

Best Practice for Success in Business Continuity

Let history and the past be a teacher to organization personnel for improving organizations' responses during emergencies and outages. Organizations' current practices and adherence to the minimum code of operation should be able to give their management and personnel confidence in their ability to deal with any emergency or crisis. Any incident or event should be analyzed to know "what went well and what did not?" It is the "what did not go well" that should be discussed further to understand areas for improvement. These would include missing capabilities, what should be changed in the current practice, etc.

As in any management initiative, it is equally important to keep improvising and improving. Such improvements can be based on the experience of the personnel, on industry best practices, and on observation. Observing refers to *how other successful organizations or their personnel do it*. While this may not be a fool-proof way to know *how competition is preparing to deal with an emergency*, it may give some indication to move in the right direction. Based on the situation and the experience, one can build a better solution that utilizes the available resources and implements more effectively.

This chapter will help the reader understand what it takes to run an effective business continuity program and what practices will aid in successful implementation of business continuity management and managing a crisis or any emergency. The non-adherence of these practices may prove to be a dampener in the management's pursuit of an effective business continuity program in the organization.

It is important for the organization to note that these various practices need to be established during the life cycle of business continuity management implementation in the organization. Some practices need to be adopted at the initiation of the program and some at a later stage when the organization gains a certain level of maturity in this domain and its employees are aware of the basics of business continuity management and what it means for them as an individual employee, at a department, or at

DOI: 10.4324/9781003304678-2

the entity level. For the ease of understanding, let us segregate these phases of business continuity implementation phases as:

1   Planning and Initiation Phase.
2   Execution and Implementation Phase.
3   Reinforcement Phase.

Planning and Initiation Phase

In this phase, the organization's management must focus their attention on addressing issues of how they will support and sustain attention for success and effectiveness of the initiative of business continuity and crisis management. As business continuity is a lesser-known domain to the staff and employees of any organization, it becomes the responsibility of the management and its leaders to proliferate the knowledge about this among the staff. This knowledge would help the staff in aiding the organization to respond to any emergency, crisis, or outage, regardless of whether the staff and employees are part of the *critical employee list* or otherwise. In both instances, the staff would need to know and be clear about their roles and responsibilities.

In doing so, the management must ensure the relevance and existence of the following:

1   Proper estimation of the financial commitment that an organization is willing to commit for the implementation of business continuity management and ongoing annual budgets for the program to be maintained effectively.
2   Proper documentation covering how the program will be administered, the five Ws and one H of the program: What, Why, When, Where, Whom, and How.
3   A comprehensive idea of the goals and scope of the business continuity policy, including what is included and what is excluded. Senior management should set the business continuity policy and objectives and ensure their alignment with the organization's business objectives and strategic plans since they typically have visibility into the organization's strategic plans, regulatory needs, and stakeholder expectations.
4   In any organization, for a governance framework for business continuity management to be effective, its management should consider deploying a cross-functional team with pertinent competencies, wherein personnel know their roles and responsibilities during a crisis in responding to strategic, tactical, and operational recovery. Its business continuity management (BCM) standard should be structured in a manner to define the roles and responsibilities in a clear manner with due clarity on personnel empowered to make a decision during a crisis/emergency.

5   Aspects relating to the requirement under the international BCM standard for the *management commitment* and its support for technically competent resources to implement and maintain the business continuity program effectively.
6   A clearly laid out document covering the roles and responsibilities under the business continuity program.
7   A comprehensive set of documentation that covers the requirements under the BCM life cycle.

The planning and initiation phase lays the basis and foundation for BCM implementation.

Cost of Planning versus the Cost of Failure

Organizations normally look at their *top line* and their *bottom line*. The top line refers to growth in revenue and financial numbers, while the bottom line refers to the costs. For companies to grow, the net differential between top line and bottom line should be a positive one that reflects increased profitability. The organization has to incur the *cost of setting up* and having BCM due to regulatory and business requirements. In both cases, the organization must balance the cost and the revenue component.

Business continuity/disaster recovery planning must be holistic in its approach for it to be realistic and effective. Stakeholders and key business personnel would need to be involved. Disaster recovery planning goes beyond recovering key technical components, while business continuity planning involves *looking forward*, anticipating disruptions, and preparing mitigating strategies for the continuity of business operations. BCM helps organizations and their management better negotiate contracts for dealing with crisis in a planned manner rather than as a reaction.

Resources: People, Process, and Technology

Planning for resources is an essential element of business continuity planning, as these will enable the organization to deploy resources during any disruption – be it people, processes, or technology.

People – It is natural human tendency that employees feel at ease and in fact more engaged in organizations that care for them and provide prospects of a secure career in the future. Having emergency procedures in place can give employees the perception that the company is well-prepared, focused on their performance, and cares about their safety. Contrary to popular belief, businesses that operate on a perpetual ad-hoc basis risk losing their most important employees for the same reason. Organizations with BC/DR Plans in place will be able to manage crisis and emergencies in a mature manner as per procedure and avoid chaos. The plans help personnel to keep calm and remain focused on the objective of resuming critical operations as soon as possible within pre-agreed RTOs (Recovery Team Objectives).

Process – The chance to assess and enhance an organization's business procedures is provided by BC/DR planning. During the business continuity implementation, operations can identify steps and activities supporting critical operations that can be "pruned and rationalized" because of proper utilization of people, improvement in processing, etc.

Technology – Scurrying to deal with technology issues once a disaster has hit is a sure shot recipe for disaster and one that can potentially cost the firm damages that could be avoided if a solid plan is in place beforehand. Contingency planning helps the organization to prepare for any outage/emergency with a "Plan B" in place that anticipates the downside impact of any disruption; thus, an organized strategy and a solution to tide over the disruption is key. Organizations can have strategic sourcing arrangements, alternate operation locations, and alternate skilled teams of staff for handling critical operations.

Execution and Implementation Phase

A well-planned approach can ease the execution and implementation of BCM. The task of executing the plan is an important turning point for the organization, as the issue of "What's in it for me?" gets addressed at all levels and with all employees of the organization. This is also important from the viewpoint that this proliferation will determine the *buy-in* for business continuity among all staff, and they will contribute to the extent of their respective roles during any future crisis or emergency. The organization personnel will be in the know of what should be done during a crisis/emergency, what role each one must play, and how the crisis will be managed effectively.

An important component of business continuity implementation is the organization having distinct segregation of its product and services that are critical or non-critical for the business of the organization. It may adopt different criteria for this segregation, namely:

1   Legacy value of the product or service.
2   Return or margin on the product or service.
3   Market share of the product or service.
4   Dominant share in the product or service portfolio of the organization, etc.
5   Any other viable parameter or any other criterion as defined by the management of the company.

These factors normally define the *BIA Parameters* on the basis of which the criticality category of any activity or function is defined, during the business impact analysis stage. These parameters must be SMART (Specific, Measurable, Achievable, Realistic and Time-bound)

Senior management is aware of the top risks and threats that keep them awake at night, so relevant stakeholders in the organization focus on regulatory requirements and constraints that affect normal performance. They must approve the risk assessment methodology for it to be successful. The risk management policy should reflect the company's culture. They must define[1] *acceptable level of risk* as a quantifiable number that can be easily understood.

Business Impact Analysis

The organization, while implementing business continuity as suggested in the international standard and in line with established BCM life cycle, should define these values as an outcome of an important phase in BCM execution and implementation by conducting a Business Impact Analysis (BIA).

The business continuity program and organization may give skewed results if the BIA approach focuses on a few key departments rather than the entire enterprise while identifying high-availability and high-cost criticalities. Senior management should consider an enterprise-level view of business functions and processes because BIA results like RTO, MBCO, and continuity strategies all have a bearing on company finances. The business continuity implementers must verify the BIA results and deal with any inconsistencies.

For these identified products and services, it is useful to know the key concepts that drive resumption and recovery of operations post disruption:

1 **RTO – Recovery Time Objective –** The period of time and service level that must elapse after a disaster (or disruption) for a business process to be restored in order to prevent unacceptable negative effects from a disruption in business continuity.
2 **MAO – Maximum Acceptable Outage –** The MAO is the time it would take after which the customer would not accept the unfavorable effects of not getting the service or product as a result of not performing a task or providing a service
3 **MBCO – Minimum Business Continuity Objective –** Minimum level of services (processes) that the company will accept in order to accomplish its goals in the event of an interruption.
4 **RPO – Recovery Point Objective –** Point at which data used by an activity must be restored for the activity to continue operating after an interruption.

These quantifiable values determine and drive the decisions for the investment required by senior management and help in strategizing the business continuity approach during any emergency or crisis. These numbers will also segregate the activities that will be resumed during a crisis and those that will be postponed. This categorization of critical and non-critical and their numerical values aid in driving the business continuity of the business units with specific recovery parameters. Organization buy-in into proper program implementation always helps if there is *top-down* senior management support.

Senior management is aware of the top risks and threats that keep them awake at night, so relevant stakeholders in the organization focus on regulatory requirements and constraints that affect normal performance. Senior management must approve the risk assessment methodology for it to be successful. The risk management policy should reflect the company's culture. They must define *acceptable level of risk* as a quantifiable number that can be easily understood.

Risk Management

The organization's long-term strategy, values, mission, and vision should guide senior management's risk assessment and risk treatment choice. Senior management must specifically approve of any residual risk if it cannot be reduced below the acceptable level.

Senior management involvement in risk management helps risk management teams and business continuity teams bond better. This alignment is crucial because the two teams act as *two sides of the same coin* during emergencies and help business units recover and resume operations within agreed timelines represented as RTOs.

Emergency Response

During this phase, the emergency response dynamics are discussed to enable time redressal of the emergency. In case it involves human injury and the need for medical attention, it becomes a priority for the organization to have proper emergency handling plans. The initial hours following a catastrophe are crucial, and it may be necessary to make quick decisions based on inadequate facts and information. Senior management's engagement at this point is essential because it guarantees the start of a proper incident response, which frequently entails trade-offs and strategic dilemmas.

The execution and implementation of business continuity in an emergency and its appropriate response with relevance of timely decisions during a crisis or emergency is important. The decisions within the first few hours can make a substantial difference in an effective response to a crisis or emergency and the lack of it, resulting in negative consequences for the organization. The right decision and action during the "Golden Hour" can indeed make a difference in human safety, protection of assets, and safeguarding of interest and reputation of the organization.

Crisis Management

Along with being able to respond to emergencies, it is crucial for the organization's staff to be able to handle any crisis situations effectively to reduce the harm that can be done to the organization's reputation, customers, market share, stakeholders, etc. The senior management plays a crucial role in shaping, leading, and developing the crisis management capabilities, which enables it to successfully implement the business continuity program and maintain the company's vital operations. Additionally, an important aspect of crisis communication is duly approved procedures while using social media effectively.

During "peace time" management should consider devising the mechanism of how the organization will deal with any crisis. There should be well-established "alert systems" that should give out signals and serve as indicators for any emerging or crisis. Senior management shapes, directs, and develops crisis management capability to fit the organization's unique requirements. Senior management leads crisis management and promotes business continuity. They should manage crisis communications and increasingly use social media.

Competency Building

The ISO 22301 Standard for Business Continuity Management and other standards require the function and responsibility of BCM to be managed by staff and employees who are competent to handle the function. This competence relates to their skill and experience in BCM to perform their role effectively following the norms and requirements as specified in Standard and regulations. The competence shall be gained by experience, training, information sharing, mentoring, *on-the-job shadowing*, etc. Senior management must ensure that post implementation of BCM in the organization, the technical capability of employees' management of the business continuity function across departments is adequate for their effective management of BCM in the organization. Senior management should identify and train for all business continuity roles and responsibilities.

Reinforcement Phase

The reinforcement phase relates to the practice of validating the "models defined in the planning/initiation phase" and the ones that get implemented for establishing "a cohesive mechanism of action steps" for organization personnel for its resiliency. This phase is all about:

Effective Communication Mechanism

A well-defined matrix for information flow and its corresponding timely decision by senior management can be crucial for the organizations' continuity and for the confidence in the organization resilience across its hierarchy. This will make it possible to respond to incidents appropriately, which is usually difficult due to strategic trade-offs.

Tests and Exercising

The relevance of tests and exercising cannot be undermined by any organization irrespective of the industry, sector, or geography. The tests and exercises give organization personnel the confidence that the plans and strategy developed to continue critical operations will stand the test of an emergency and crisis, and business shall be restored and resumed within the defined and approved recovery time objectives while limiting the losses for the organization and protecting its personnel and its market share and reputation. Properly conducted tests and exercises yield the *chinks in the armor* of crisis and emergency response and bring out fallacies in the plans. These also brings out what is not working well in the plan, and its analysis points out what needs to change or be improvised so that business can be conducted uninterrupted. Over a period of time, different types of tests and exercises should be completed so that all aspects of test plans get validated for their effectiveness and all the staff become aware of their respective roles and responsibilities during and post crisis.

Management Reviews

Management reviews reinforce management's commitment to BCM to be successfully implemented across the organization. Although much has changed in the last two decades with respect to BCM being an evolving science, organizations and their managements are ploughed with multiple options for an effective and specific solution that will address the fulfill-ment of organization business continuity objectives. As the *Sponsor of a Business ContinuityProgram,* the CEO, along with his/her senior man-agement team, should pay more attention to the planning dimension of the BCM process than that of the implementation, as the output of plans provides a tangible response while effectiveness of preparations is only known in the event of the organization invoking the continuity plans.

The management should be able to see the full circle, right from initi-ation, to planning, to implementation, to operational management. The operational management should have the components of incident man-agement and testing. Incident management will have end-to-end capa-bility of incident response, emergency management, crisis management, crisis communication, and business continuity. The management review should, at regular intervals, reinforce these arrangements as also these should be validated through periodic audits.

Continual Improvement

Senior management should endeavor to improve business continuity effectiveness through policy, objectives, internal audit, independent review, testing and exercising, and management review. In the BCM journey of any organization, its culture and the behavior of all employees should be "BCM centric," by which it is meant that business continuity as a focus and day-to-day norm is understood by staff and practiced by them. With this culture change, the need for constantly striving for improvement in the BCM pro-gram should be practiced by all employees.

Budget for BCM

It is primarily the responsibility of the senior management to ensure that enough resources and budgets are allocated for effective maintenance of the business continuity program in the organization. The budget acts as the *fuel and oil for the BCM machine*, where various aspects of the business continuity life cycle require funds and resources for accomplishing the objectives set out in the business continuity program. The multifarious requirements and need for funds are palpable to run such an initiative in any organization, if the business continuity is to be implemented in a proper manner following the minimum prescribed practices as detailed in the International Business Continuity Standard – ISO 22301 and other local standards in this domain.

A duly approved adequate budget ensures the initiatives of hiring and deploying competent/appropriately skilled and experienced resources as well as training in the business continuity domain after a due *training need analysis* that establishes the current level of crisis preparedness and its desired level. Different levels of training require different levels of en-gagement of staff and correspond to the cost and depth of training ses-sions. Apart from training, the business continuity program requires the management to provide for factors enabling BCM implementation, for example, cost of the promotional campaign, proliferation material, cost of gifts and giveaways, etc. The availability of funds also provides options to the BCM team to explore means for more effective implementation of BCM and add resilience to the organization.

Conclusion

From the three phases of business continuity implementation – the Planning and Initiation Phase, the Execution and Implementation Phase, and the Reinforcement Phase – it can be observed that for a BCMS to be effectively implemented involves a systematic approach, management commitment, adequate funding, and skilled resources having the right experience to understand the vagaries of the business environment and *adjust the business continuity management framework of the organization to counter these risks and threats.*

The organization and its management must think through how the business continuity program will be structured in order to protect the interests of the entity as a result of any disruption. Management should devise mechanisms that recognize the risks and threats that can hamper its operations and cause adverse financial impacts, damage its reputation, alter its market share, and result in a negative impact for its customers. Business continuity planning and IT DR preparedness help organizations in countering these threats and give their personnel the confidence to face any crisis or emergency. The personnel in organizations with BC DR plans are trained to act in a responsible manner; their actions are akin to their respective roles and responsibilities as per documented processes.

The structured plans help the organization with due commitment and support from senior management, which ensures a *top-down participative approach to BCM implementation.* Such an approach ensures better chances of effectiveness of the business continuity program. It also ensures that employees having a role in organization BCMS and will act more responsibly in case of any crisis with an over-all buy-in across the organization. This highlights to the organization the downside of not having business continuity readiness.

Key Take-Aways

- Every incident, especially the ones with negative impacts, should be analyzed for lessons learned. An opportunity exists to adopt corrective measures for better handling of similar incidents that may come.
- A thought-through approach to business continuity management implementation will indeed have better chances of success than one based on an ad-hoc approach.
- A top-down implementation approach has been observed to yield better effectiveness results for business continuity programs.

- The right identification of critical and non-critical operations based on right *Business Impact Parameters* is an important milestone in the BCM journey of the organization.
- A badly performed *Business Impact Analysis* can have a catastrophic effect on the implementation of a business continuity program in the organization and its corresponding success.

Chapter 3

Selecting a BCM Tool
Imperatives and Prime Considerations

In this chapter, we look at the prime considerations for selecting a business continuity management (BCM) tool. The significance of organizational BCM maturity before a tool is deployed is important. An improper strategy of business continuity automation can spell a recipe for failure and a colossal waste of effort, money, and other resources and may result in compromised organization resiliency.

Identifying the needs of the organization will determine the expanse of the BCM tool selection and deployment. The organization also needs to *take stock* of the capabilities of its current people, existing processes, and current technical prowess of teams to this along with available technology in dealing with situations, especially during an emergency and outage.

It is believed that *necessity is the mother of invention*, yet there have been ample examples in history that have proved that this may not always be true. In certain cases, despite a demand being there, it has taken some time for mankind to realize the need for making the demand meet the supply.

Organizations across the globe need to address the key questions for stakeholders:

A   Are we resilient as an organization?
B   Is the organization ready to respond effectively to a crisis or emergency?
C   Are the organization personnel *crisis ready*?

The organization and its management need to determine in a realistic manner the answers to these questions. In today's dynamic world impacted by social, economic, and political uncertainties, organizations need to do a realistic assessment to know if they are prepared to face a crisis or disruption and whether there are obvious cracks in the organizational resilience edifice. The answers to the questions above can be used as the basis by which senior management and leaders may assess the current capability of the organization to respond to any emergency, outage, or disruption and recover from it in an effective manner.

DOI: 10.4324/9781003304678-3

History has shown that managements that have been successful in *bouncing back* are companies that have practiced *preparing for the uncertain* and visualizing the after effects of any emergency/crisis and taking effective measures to overcome the problem. These organizations have in some way or another implemented and practiced BCM – either wholly or partially in its implementation across the organization. Traditionally, organizations used to deploy simple manual procedures and practices to address the need for BCM; however, as times changed, organizations' growth momentum increased, and organizations grew substantially in their market share, their customer base grew, and their balance sheet size grew leaps and bounds, it became increasingly troublesome to manage the business continuity using traditional means, which were primarily through the use of a Word document or an Excel file.

BCM becomes difficult to manage due to business complexity and environment. CEOs, COOs, CXOs, CTOs, and senior management should plan for emergencies, crises, and outages in today's volatile business environment to minimize damage to their company's reputation, customers, stakeholders, and market status. The COVID-19 pandemic, cyber threats, and supply chain disruptions have alerted managers and senior management to these uncertainties. Technology, when used smartly, can be used to automate long, tedious manual processes by reducing dependency on human memory, manual processes, and human actions, thereby avoiding harm to stakeholders.

To bring about a significant change that challenges the normal routine or introduces a new way of doing the same thing, it is important to have knowledge of what one wants to change or its impact. The organization's DNA must be well ingrained in a technical solution to transform BCM and its implementation in accordance with the applicable rules, regulations, and prescriptive compliance as per ISO 22301, the International Standard for Business Continuity Management Systems, implying that the BCM solution is well proliferated in the organization's daily work routine.

For BCM to be successfully implemented in any organization, it is important that it is ready to incorporate the BCMS methodology and that its personnel realize the significance of such an exercise at the entity level for its overall benefits and advantages to all the organization stakeholders. The organization should have matured management information systems across the span of the organization that can be duly amalgamated with the new BCMS. As the other organization management information systems (MIS) are aligned to its vision, mission, and values, the same should be the objective of the BCMS as well.

Staff readiness across the hierarchy is another indicator of an organization's readiness to automate its BC capability. "What is BCM? How is it beneficial to themselves and the company? What constitutes a crisis?

When will this methodology be invoked, and what would be their specific role and responsibility?" should be known to all staff. The answers to these seemingly innocuous questions may determine how the organization and its people handle a crisis or disruption with ease and success or with difficulty and failing in protecting the interest of the organization.

Another key imperative for tool decision is the issue of BCM tool technology mapping with the existing technology already in use. This also determines whether existing investment in technology solution can be usefully supplemented while deploying the BCM tool or will be an additional investment in the latest technology for getting optimal returns with the use of new and advanced technical solutioning. The compatibility of the tool, its customization to the organization's requirements, and its ability to meet future requirements through version updates and source code enhancement should also be cleared with the tool provider to avoid any confusion and chaos later. These are best managed when the same are incorporated in the contract or the Service Level Agreement (SLA).

Identifying the needs of the organization will determine the expanse of the BCM tool selection and its deployment. The organization also needs to take stock of the capabilities of its current staff, existing processes, and current technical prowess of teams to utilize its people, its processes, and available technology in dealing with situations, especially in a *crunch time* situation, i.e., during an emergency and outage.

Purpose and Objective of Automation

At the management level and corresponding operating level, it is crucial to have clarity of what is the organizational requirement that the automation and software will contribute towards BCM requirement. It is important to search for the right software to accomplish the objective of organization resiliency. Selecting a simple-to-implement and easy-to-understand business continuity product that will be utilized in customers' single site operation or their multiple locations across geographies must be considered comprehensively.

While the primary objective of some customers is to automate the administration of the BCM program, other users require a kind of notification or a message detailing the incident, which should be triggered by the software with due human input that provides reports and MIS reports after due analysis and reporting capabilities. The number of people making the business continuity team and their functional responsibilities also determine whether the supplier-offered solution meets the organization's needs or whether further customization of the tool is needed to be able to meet the organization's specific requirements. Upon knowing and understanding the organization's critical operations, one can decide on the prioritization of activities and functions that the tool needs to support.

Age of the Tool

It is essential to learn about the period the product has been available to customers before one can comprehend the nature of the experience that organizations have had when utilizing the system. The age of the tool can be a good reference check point for its acceptability based on the number of customers using it and its duration. If the tool has a strong presence in the market, the BCM tool and supporting system are likely to be more reliable and consistent, having been in use by a large number of users and customers. On the other hand, will your organization be utilizing the most recent technology and having the best possible user experience?

The use of the latest available technology could be a solution that has incorporated the shortcomings of the earlier versions and the new emerging requirements for effectiveness of the tool. It is essential to consider the new software for its benefits and drawbacks associated with being an early user. During the start-up phase, the organization may find a fantastic initial price and obtain some great new interfaces or technology, but it also runs the risk and downside of dealing with a lot of frequent updates and changes for a while.

For new products to establish themselves in the market, it typically takes several months, if not years, of ongoing testing and updating. It may be prudent to inquire about the customers of the tool provider with whom they currently work with, how long they have been working with them, and whether the clients are known to have a history of issues. It may be a good idea to have some insight into system issues and challenges through an open discussion with the provider. Any awards to their name can also be a good reference check.

Original Tool Provider (OTP) and Re-Seller

One important facet in any decision involving purchase of a BCM tool is the relevance of the original tool provider and their duly *authorized re-seller*. Both parties are driven by different considerations in the sale of the tool. Are the re-sellers merely a software provider or do they also offer consulting and training services in business continuity? The aftersale implementation and consulting are critical for the customer; this will also lay the robust foundation of the tool being properly embedded with due *technical feasibility* in line with other applications and systems deployed in the organization. It is critical for organization to consider the training of its personnel on the tool and awareness of its features, functionalities, and tips for troubleshooting. A sample demo of the tool may not necessarily cover the objective, focus, and the *pain points* of the customer organization when it comes to continuing the critical operations during an emergency or any disruption.

The customer should be able to discern from the offerings of the tool provider whether the tool will serve the objective of enhancing the organization resiliency or will be another additional system that is only form filling the requirement of business continuity.

Objectivity

Organizations should actively deliberate the objectives they endeavor to achieve through the deployment of the BCM tool and whether the tool will be a *good fit* in the cultural DNA of the organization. The managers and the personnel involved in the decision making for the selection of the right BCM tool should know the specific requirement and purpose that the tool will address.

These personnel should be familiar with the weak links in the current chain of organization resilience. They should be aware of the missing factors that risk a stable organization resilience status and expose *chinks in the armor* that can prove fatal to the organization's ability to continue its critical operations. As seasoned BCM practitioners, they should ensure that the tool fulfills the purpose and has the following basic functionalities:

- User interface being straight forward and easy to understand
- Incorporated the so-called "Best Practices" in the BCM domain
- Provides visual dashboards for easy understanding
- Includes specialized capability for BIAs, plans, risk assessments, exercises, and reporting to cover the entirety of the business continuity life cycle
- Adequacy of storage space for the supporting documents and its seamless access and functioning of the tool
- Incorporates the use of automated reminders in the system for administrative chores such as plan updates and review schedules, etc.
- Provide some type of portable access to plans via mobile applications or anything similar if there is a disruption
- Offer an effective data analytics function that includes reports using graphical representation
- Maintain stringent guidelines regarding data security and user privacy for all users
- Makes it possible to access the system in a secure manner from any device, regardless of its location

Acquaintance with the Tool

The customer organization and its personnel using the tool should be aware about the tool features and functionalities, and this could be achieved by a face-to-face meeting between customer and tool provider or a virtual meeting over the Internet. Both these have their pluses and minuses, as detailed in Table 3.1, as shown hereunder:

Table 3.1 Understanding Tool Features: Basis of Customer Interaction with Provider

Face-to-Face Meeting	Meeting over the Internet
Information that is more in-depth all at once	Less time-consuming
Inquires immediately and directly on the spot	Provides a useful summary of the most important aspects
Establishes a rapport with them and has faith in their expertise	Gives you the ability to view at your own convenience
Determines whether they are located onshore or overseas	Reiterates the crucial aspects to your most critical stakeholders

As a prospective customer, the organization personnel may decide on the medium to understand the features and detailing of the tool's capability, its robustness, and its ability to meet organization objectives. It is significant to note that the medium chosen should be in line and in sync with the organization's culture and its DNA.

The version number of the tool is reflective of the number of iterations the tool has undergone while meeting the evolving requirements of the customers. The versions incorporate points of changes as required by the customer or for any regulatory compliance. Corollary to the version is the aspect of scope of upgrade of technology as per the latest developments in technology.

Training and User Profiles

The *"proof of the pudding is in the eating,"* meaning one can only know if something is good or bad by trying it or using it. The organization personnel who will be ultimately benefited by the BCM tool should be aware of how to use it effectively. This highlights an important point: That the staff responsible for maintaining and contributing to business continuity function should be aware of how to operate the tool and its related functionalities. For this to happen, the relevant staff must be trained on the tool features and its functions.

The organization may invest in the best BCM tool, but it may not serve the full purpose if its complete functionalities if not put to use by staff over a period of time, and in fact, with elapse of time the very same staff may disregard the tool due to other work priorities. The BCM manager, along with the department head, should be able to discern who among the staff will be allocated the different privileges in the usage of the tool and its staff configuration. This means that it is necessary to have an understanding of the user profiles that are necessary to administer your system and the requirements in the business continuity program.

Every system is unique, but in general, one will need administrators who have full access to the system, team members who may need read-only access to their plans, plan owners and/or maintainers would need edit rights, and general staff may simply be registered in the system for contact purposes. Having administrators who have full access to the system is a requirement. After that, the organization needs to design a training program that is appropriate because these users will interact with the system and the business continuity plan.

It is essential, considering the preferences of the organization, to understand the type of training solution that will be most appropriate for its users. It is imperative that this aspect be taken into consideration before a choice is made if on-site training is something that is vital; however, if you go with an international tool provider, this may not always be available. It is recommended to conduct training for the system's more active users in person, preferably in small groups, and over a period of several days or weeks. This can frequently take a significant amount of time up front.

There are also a few things to think about if e-learning is chosen as a mode of training for "light users" or refreshers, which is becoming increasingly common. It is important to make sure that the training is simple to comprehend, and that the terminology is easily understood by the person who will be using it. E-learning is a fantastic alternative for geographically distributed teams, as well as for frequent refresher training and new staff members, because it eliminates the need for them to wait for the next on-site training session to take place. In many cases, it is also the most cost-efficient method of training available.

Tool Cost

Different types and different sized organizations have varied requirements when it comes to selecting an appropriate BCM tool. There are several important factors that need to be considered from the standpoint of an organization's BCM requirement and the tool features and functionalities that should complement these requirements.

The organization should address the following issues when deciding to purchase a BCM tool:

- Number of locations in scope, which will determine the number of licenses.
- Number of users who will use the tool and their profiles, be it read-only access, editable rights, or full access rights of tool administration.
- Whether the architecture of the tool is in sync with the organization set-up.
- The tool dashboards and reports are compatible to other MIS.
- The customization of the tool for meeting current and future needs of the organization in respect of business continuity capability or its enhancement.
- Tool compatibility with other technology being used in the organization.

From the above listed factors for the cost of BCM tools, tools with specific features and functionality are priced differently, and these also corelate to the reality of multiple tool options available in the market. BCM tools, like any other technology product, typically have the following cost composition:

Total Cost of BCM Tool =

+ Tool Cost (primarily relates to the platform, technology and development),.. **30%**

+ Implementation Cost (all cost and expenses related to implementation and installation costs for BCM tool deployment),.. **15%**

+ Infrastructure Cost, if any (to host the tool),.. **10%**

+ AMC Cost (Annual Maintenance Contract cost payable to provider for support and maintenance of the BCM tool),.. **15%**

+ User License for Location (in case of tool deployment at independent entities or locations for the organization automating BCM),

+ User License for Users (based on number of Users with different privileges and access rights), .. **20%**

+ Training Cost, if any (for upskilling client personnel on the use, features, and functionalities of the BCM tool), and.. **10%**

+ Any other costs agreed between tool provider and
prospective customer (example cost of customization of tool as per requirement, incorporation of
company logo, any specific requirement for reports,
incorporating corporate logo, look and feel of dashboards, etc.).

> .. Cost driven
> by customer
> specific
> requirement &
> change
> required on
> Source Code

Management in the organization should also see that the cost of the tool is
economical and cost-effective and is one that it can afford without putting
strain on the overall budget. The cost also must consider the need for and
requirement of tool software development and improvement. The cost of
software upgrades and version change requirements should also be considered in the overall cost and planning for the future. Forward-looking
organizations may also consider building the development skills internally
within their teams and may even buy-out the *Source Code* of the software
supporting the BCM tool. This strategy of backward integration is of
immense utility to large organizations who have the financial muscle to
undertake this step.

Ease of Understanding and Implementation over a Definite Period

Another key consideration for the management and organization going in
for BCM automation should be the ease of implementing the tool in its
entirety over a definite period – to yield the desired outcome of spending.
It is important that the organization achieves this for its twin objectives of
getting the optimum return on their investment over a period and the tool
adding to the company's resiliency to prepare it for facing any emergency
or crisis.

The above has two significant facets: That organization personnel
should understand *how the tool is structured* and *how that structure is
mapped to its organization structure*. Both these aspects will help the BCM
stakeholder in the organization to understand the effectiveness and success of the implementation of the BCM tool in the organization. This
further implies that staff should understand the BCM tool in a manner that
they are able to corelate the documentary and compliance aspect within
the offerings and "menu options" of the BCM tool. Upon understanding
this important aspect, data gathering and data collation using the BCM tool
will also be of the right quality and will serve the right purpose during a
crisis/emergency when the BCM tool functionalities "kick-in" when the
business continuity plan is invoked during an emergency or crisis.

It is significant that the tool reports and outputs during an emergency
and/or crisis are such that they help the management to make a sound

decision. This vital aspect is one that should be considered in the planning stage prior to purchase of the BCM tool. The management of the organization must be clear of what it would require by way of information and inputs from across the departments and operations to enable it to make a decision regarding continuity of the organization's critical operations during an emergency and crisis.

Conclusion

Business continuity as a domain is still an evolving action-based science. There are several factors that have contributed to organizations and senior management in companies across the world realizing its value and its contribution to organization resilience. Organizations have experienced its value through structured response during emergency and crisis; planned coordination through well-established plans during confusion and chaos; sending the right communication with the right message to protect organizational interests and reputation; protecting the interests of employees and customers in unison with optimal spending, thus yielding savings for the organization; etc.

The Covid pandemic, issues with cyber security and cyber threats, the increased supply chain management risk, rapid digitization, issues resulting from the Suez Canal blockade, urgent demands for enhanced information security, and many other recent developments and events have exposed organizations' capacity to "sail through" emergencies and prosper in times of crisis. Such occurrences have also compelled enterprises to question whether they should put all of their organizational resiliency eggs in one basket.

Organizations, leaders, and all staff members must be aware of the risk of uncertainty and should be prepared with Plans C and D in case of an emergency, while maintaining Plan B as the organization's obvious business continuity plan strategy at the unit, section, or department level, as well as at the organizational level. The use of "technology as an enabler" by businesses should be prioritized in order to replace the time-consuming manual processes, no matter how sound and established they may be.

It is common knowledge that technology, when used effectively, will increase the efficiency of the process, systems, products, and services and result in the desired outcome being achieved while also streamlining processes, maintaining data flow, and maintaining its integrity. This also helps in reducing the cost and impacts positive and sustainable growth. From the above, it can be stated with conviction that an organization and its management must consider the option of taking a BCM tool as a very careful decision.

Key Take-Aways

- Examine deeply whether an organization is ready to implement automation in business continuity function.
- Does the organization have matured plans and processes to handle crisis, emergencies, and disruption effectively PRIOR to its ability to continue its critical operations?
- Understand the maturity of the organization with respect to its business continuity readiness and its effectiveness for automation to succeed.
- Are the organization personnel, processes, and technology in sync to undertake the initiative of introduction of new business continuity tool technology?
- Will automation succeed in a definite timeline based on the organization's current culture?
- Ensure the organization has its "laundry list of requirements" of what the BCM tool will deliver on demand.
- Final decision for selection of a particular BCM tool – who decides and what criterion?

Chapter 4

Capital Considerations for Assessing BCM Requirement

In this chapter, we cover the requirements of capital considerations for the Board/senior management when embarking on the business continuity journey for the organization. Questions include: How much should we invest in this initiative? What are the deciding factors and the basis for the program and its essential requirements with respect to experienced personnel? What training and awareness are required for its effective implementation and essentials for maintaining the business continuity program? What is the currency of its documentation and adherence to the statutes and regulations for business continuity?

Based on the far-reaching impact of disruptions and outages, it is important for organizations to set aside and invest in Plan B and Plan C for ensuring continuity of what the organization considers as critical, Plan A being the obvious course of action to be followed during any contingency. The value of the investment is also impacted by "risk to be covered" and having the right combination of people and technology, process and technology, and clarity about the expected outcome of the business continuity requirements.

One of the major dilemmas for management and senior leaders is to consider the costs and benefits of business continuity management (BCM), whether it is an investment in the company's balance sheet or a liability. The public reasoning is why should the company invest in something that may not contribute any revenue for the company's bottom line and protect against something that hopefully may not happen. It is somewhat like insurance; however, in insurance, the contingent event (against which insurance is taken) must occur for insurable benefits to be realized, while in business continuity the organization may utilize the benefits of its investment even in the absence of any real crisis or emergency.

The proponents of BCM maintain that its benefit may yield positivity without any adversity being faced by the company. Such benefits could be improvement in operations, better utilization of resources, and process

DOI: 10.4324/9781003304678-4

improvements as a way of doing business or knowing what to do and how to conduct operations when facing an emergency or crisis in the company.

The BCM literature fails to adequately address this topic, even though it is essential to the practice of business continuity and crisis management as a professional domain. Most of the international standards, guidelines, and regulations do not cover this aspect directly when it comes to the prime responsibility of selling or proliferating business continuity internally within the organization and as to who should be attributed for its success in the organization. This is also primarily since in most organizations its ownership is not clearly defined other than that "the CEO, as the key sponsor, is responsible for its implementation" from a regulatory standpoint.

Due to the distributed nature of tasks and activities required to be performed during a crisis, emergency, or disruption, there are *action steps* required to be executed by teams from human resources (to care for employees, their extended family, the welfare of the impacted staff, etc.), from IT (to ensure constant IT and technology connectivity within pre-agreed recovery time objectives [RTOs] and to use technology *as an enabler*), from administration and the logistics teams (to facilitate a shift of operations from primary site to alternate work area recovery site, arrangement at alternate site, etc.), from operations (to ensure continuity of critical operations), from the finance team (to ensure availability of funds for dealing with a crisis or emergency), from the procurement team (for ensuring urgent procurement to support a critical part of operations), from the legal team (for issuing a legal statement concerning 360 degrees of stakeholder interest, to handle media, etc.). The above listed are only a few of the examples of the complexity that organizations may face during a crisis or emergency; hence, it is prudent for managements of organizations to invest in business continuity implementation. It is also due to this diversity of requirements during an emergency and crisis that managements face the dilemma to identify a *clear owner of business continuity in the organization.*

BCM emphasizes hard and soft skills equally. To clarify, hard skills are technical skills and the ability to perform specific tasks needed for a job. Experience gives this skill. The job description (JD) or job postings usually list hard skills, which seem vague. Formal training helps acquire hard skills. On-the-job, dedicated, online, and certification programs teach business continuity hard skills. When organizations and their management start a BCM journey, they must choose the right skilled and experienced resources for the specific tasks under the business continuity life cycle for each task in the life cycle. This would require budgeting for staff business continuity training and certification.

Along with the hard skills, experienced resource management and handling of business continuity also require soft skills, which are attributable to individual personality traits that impact interpersonal interactions and productivity. Soft skills have an important role in effectiveness of individuals and their success within the group dynamics. Some of these skills that are important for success in business continuity and the crisis management domain are as follows:

- Analytical skills.
- Communication and influencing skills.
- Collaboration and adaptability.
- Inter-personal skills.
- Being technology savvy.

It is pertinent to note that while these hard and soft skills play an important role in the success of the business continuity program in any organization, there is little realization of how these skills aid in expediting the BCM journey for the organization. It is for leaders to recognize this *missing part* in the personnel and teams entrusted with the responsibility of business continuity and crisis management implementation and provide for funds required to upskill the staff. These skills help the people working in BCM to be better trainers, better analysts, better communicators, and better presenters and influencers.

BCM is commonly associated with problem situations for the organization, wherein the failure is attributed to high expense during an emergency and outage and lack of the right investment, which could have reduced or limited the excesses and wastage. This again reverts to the point of whether BCM is an expense or an investment for the organization. COVID-19 jolted management teams in most organizations across the globe into realizing that planning for the uncertain does help with savings and reducing/limiting the exposure or else it will be a difficult situation for the organization after a crisis. COVID-19 has highlighted that financial planning from the aspect of uncertainty is vital for budgetary planning. The last two–three years have highlighted the relevance of the following factors:

- Need for more coordinated operations.
- Realignment of "management priorities."
- Continuous financial planning and reassessment.
- Increased cost of doing normal business.
- Fast track the *"Digital Transformation for Organizations."*
- Dynamism to inculcate agility in the business environment.

It will be observed that all the points listed above have a significant impact on the costs and finances of the organization, and the same needs to be planned and budgeted for if the organization has to survive and also prepare itself for tomorrow. This requires a very critical analysis of the many aspects with financial implications for the entity. As an outcome of Covid and the changed business environment, organizations need to consider the following carefully in their budgetary planning process:

- Increased cost of doing business.
- Need for quick management decisions, especially involving finance.
- Relook at finance and costs.
- Cost associated with additional regulatory compliance.
- Increased IT-related and IT infrastructure costs.

The business continuity manager or the BCM team should ensure that all elements related to business continuity effectiveness are considered in their true relevance when the annual budgets are being planned.

It is equally important to note that some of these capital expenditures may not be required in the future as once the pandemic risks and threats have been recognized and dealt with, these may suffice if any other pandemic were to re-occur. Hence, the budgeting exercise should consider the current and future requirements accordingly.

It is surprising that organizations and management only "wake up" when internal and external auditors point out resilience-based risks and threats. Auditors usually highlight "regulatory requirements and risks associated with actual practices." Business continuity with proper alignment of people, processes, and technology can help management teams avoid such situations. This will also prevent "knee-jerk" reactions to emergency situations that require "coughing up extraneous financial resources to tide over uncertainty." Thus, of the above changes, organizational culture change would be the most significant and likely the most long-term. Traditional change management experts estimate that any organization culture changes in over five years under normal conditions. Organizations today need a two- to three-year change management program with accelerators in a fast-changing world with risks. This requires leadership commitment, stewardship, and workforce engagement.

Most organizations and their management partake in BCM to meet only the mandatory regulatory and legal requirement that are required to have a continuity strategy for their critical part of the operations. In following these mandatory statutes, organizations normally invest the basic and minimum to meet the regulation and to adhere to the law so as not to get a non-compliance finding in audits. While this stance on the part of the organization is fine, it is fine only if it does not result in a "form filling exercise," which has been seen as a common occurrence in many organizations.

Corporate history is riddled with many instances where, despite adequate investments in business continuity and crisis management, the organizations have had to face major losses, outages, impact on reputation, and dissatisfied customers. It is important to understand that *allocating and spending money on business continuity has to be equally backed-up by its proper monitoring and effective implementation*. A well-implemented business continuity program, on the other hand, ensures adherence to legal and compliance requirements as well as protects the interest of all stakeholders: Employees, customers, management, vendors and suppliers, service providers, etc.

The benefits and advantages of investing in business continuity are important because the organization is preparing for something uncertain that may or may not benefit it. Organization culture, people, processes, and DNA affect these benefits. These characteristics of the organization also determine the degree of success for a new initiative like BCM as BCM's governance, implementation, monitoring, and effectiveness depend on the organization's people, process synchronization, and corporate willingness to be crisis ready.

BCM implementation success depends on how quickly management decisions are implemented and followed. Organizational culture is crucial. Organizations that recognize the importance of being prepared for any crisis or emergency can take advantage of "The Golden Hour" and gain control of the situation faster than their competitors. Organizations that benefit and capitalize on such opportunities realize the better value of investment in BCM.

The leaders and managers of such enterprises pro-actively prepare their organization and staff to answer the following questions: "What should we concentrate on during an emergency and disruption?" "What should we do or not do?" "What should we do to continue the critical operations of the company?" These aspirational objectives for the management and leaders do not come cheap, and the management must ensure that the right efforts, inputs, and resources are put in to yield the desired outcome.

Forward-looking and progressive leadership of enterprises realize that success in business continuity during "crunch time" should have the following in place:

- Skilled and experienced staff in the BCM domain.
- Adequate budget and funding for the business continuity program.
- Governance and implementation framework.

For all these to be in place, there should be enough advanced planning and execution. Skilled and experienced staff in the BCM domain are quite sought after, especially after the COVID-19 pandemic – as Covid has made organizations deal with situations that were unprecedented, and most countries were not ready to face the scale and enormity of the pandemic. The role of experienced and knowledgeable personnel in business continuity ensures that organizations can do better planning and there are more robust action steps and strategies to enable the organization to continue its critical operations. The critical part of the operations is duly identified end-to-end with the resource requirement, internal and external dependencies, the recovery time objective, the technology requirement, dependency on service providers, etc. These are well covered when any organization embarks on the business continuity journey.

As a prerequisite, any important initiative or program requires management support with due backing for its finance and monetary requirements. It is important that organization managements should allocate adequate funds and budget based on the nature of its operation, number of staff, and locations within the scope of this program, and the depth of BCM concepts and their awareness among employees across the organizational hierarchy.

Coupled with the requirement of resources and funding, it is also required that these two aspects be supported by a clear and comprehensive governance model. This will ensure the management thrust in the implementation of the business continuity program and reiterate the value of readiness for any emergency situation or disruption. The formal governance framework ensures that all personnel in the entity are aware of the significance of the five Ws and one H during any emergency or crisis. The five Ws are: What, When, Where, Why, and by Whom, and the H is for How.

Another critical factor that the Board of Directors and senior leaders in the organization need to be cognizant of, is the growing span of risk and threats emerging due to the social, economic, and political environment across the globe. Along with these are the risks due to cyber security breach, supply chain risk management (SCRM), rapid advancement in technology and the high pace of digitization, risk due to data theft, etc. From the plethora of these risks and threats, it is prudent that the organization invest in business continuity and crisis planning to prepare the organization to be crisis ready with its staff duly aware of their To Dos during an emergency and outage.

Conclusion

In the last decade or so, there has been an increasing realization that the Boards and management teams in organizations need to be ready for any emergency, crisis, or outage, irrespective of its duration. Since 2020, organizations have been exposed to risks due to a pandemic of a global scale and how operations of enterprises across countries and continents could be paralyzed at the same time and in such abundance. These challenges have forced management teams to *think-through* and come out with smarter solutions in the wake of these new risks, threats, and hazards.

The pace of response to these threats and risks that have emerged has also impacted the nature and behavior of people in dealing with these risks. They have adopted a faster pace of digitalization to enable the use of technology and its prowess. The "digital revolution" of the last two–three years has catapulted the perception and application of technology solutions and their corresponding investment. These investments in technology are also driven by the fact that the ultimate goal of enabling technology is to ensure the continuity of an organization's critical operations, which will keep it sustained even in times of adversity. It is for this reason that management and senior leaders in companies and organizations plan for investing in business continuity and to take advantages of its implementation, thereby saving crucial and limited financial resources and getting the optimal return on investment (ROI). The leaders need to keep considered decision keeping in mind the interests of various stakeholders, along with the aspect of regulatory requirements and compliance.

The investment in business continuity and crisis management must be followed with the right infusion and its proliferation across all levels of organization hierarchies. The success of business continuity implementation is dependent on several internal and external factors, and it is of relevance how the managements in companies can devise and develop the business continuity governance framework, its policy and documentation, its awareness among the employees, the knowledge of key roles and responsibilities for effective emergency and crisis management, etc. The management should ensure it has a *mechanism to measure the pulse and effectiveness of business continuity implementation*. All these aspects need to be considered in detail by the Boards and senior leaders prior to embarking on the business continuity journey and at the time when the organization wants to *automate business continuity*. The automation of business continuity is a more deep-rooted decision by the management, duly covered in the chapter "Selecting a BCM Tool – Imperatives and Prime Considerations."

Key Take-Aways

- Organizations need to have a plan for all probable risks and threats they envisage in the short, medium, and long term.
- Investment in BCM should be a considered decision by the Board of Directors or senior leaders.
- Once embarking on the business continuity journey, it is generally an irreversible action, as this requires considerable expense if done in the right manner.
- Other than the requirement of funds for investment in business continuity, also required are as follows:

- ○ Hard skills for ensuring that tasks are performed to maintain effective business continuity.
- ○ Soft skills play a key role in the success of BCM through inter-play of group dynamics where a number of people and parties are involved in its implementation.
- ○ Coordination across the organization to have unified action during an emergency, crisis, or outage, and so on.
- ○ Defined list of priorities for the continuity of critical operations.
- ○ Knowing the financial numbers that impact operations, e.g., sales per day/per week/per month, cost per unit, cost of downtime, direct and indirect costs, etc.
- ○ Knowledge of market dynamics, its market share, what the competition is doing, forecasting market demand, etc., in relation to their preparedness for any emergency or crisis.

- Regulatory and legal compliance should not be the "drivers for implementing business continuity" in the organization; the interest of the organization and its staff should be the prime drivers.
- Investment in business continuity should keep pace with the changes in technology and best practices in its automation over a reasonable period.

Chapter 5

"Peace Time" Initiatives for Organization Management

In this book and in business continuity management (BCM) as a domain being promoted, "peace time initiatives" prepare organizations and their staff for any crises or emergency. Organizational management faces many different situations that require their attention, such as a financial decision, an urgent procurement, a supply chain risk management issue, the impact of an external real-time incident, or the impact on a key customer for any reason. Management decisions and timing are crucial in these and other everyday situations. Management makes these decisions based on the organization's vision and mission, stakeholders' interests, customers and market share, financial viability, operational feasibility, market capital impact, and other factors relevant in view of the perception of individual management personnel.

In this chapter, we will discuss some key considerations during "non-crisis" periods, when organization efforts can be more objectively driven and its crisis plans and strategies can be meaningfully validated. Risk assessment and operational dependencies can be better explored without the pressure of a crisis. Peace time allows the company and its personnel to consider its business options and choose a favorable, optimal, and cost-effective strategy.

While there can be a number of initiatives that an organization and its management can consider for the continuity of its operations, especially the critical part within a predefined time period, some of the key initiatives that any management should pursue during the normal business-as-usual (BAU) conditions are listed here:

1 **Test and Exercise of Various Plans** – With the increase of risks and threats and the advent of technology, there is a pressing need for the management of organizations to look into the critical issue of continuity of operations should any of these risks or threats materialize in reality, as organizations have multi-prong approaches to deal with these risk factors and have different plans to address the downside of these risks.

DOI: 10.4324/9781003304678-5

Although these plans may be called by different names, the primary concerns these plans tend to cover for the organization are listed here:

a Incident Management.
b Emergency Response.
c Crisis Management.
d Crisis Communication.
e Business Continuity.
f IT Disaster Recovery.
g Media Response.
h Stakeholder Management.
i Emergency Procurement, etc.

The important aspect of these plans in any organization is their "ownership": Who is supposed to keep them updated and current, who will ensure that the plans and personnel are in sync for the right response during a crisis or emergency, what is senior management's onus with regards to these different plans, who in the organization will ensure that these different plans can commonly address the needs of the organization during any crisis or emergency, how will these plans get activated and coordinated, etc.

It is for these reasons that senior management and organization personnel must ensure that when it comes to evidencing the resiliency of the organization it should not be that *"it is a paper tiger"* with all aspects duly covered ONLY in the documented plans, procedures, and standard operating procedures. Accordingly, all the plans in the organization must:

- Be clearly documented with their versions and review date clearly incorporated.
- Have details of the "owner."
- Have a clearly laid-down basis of the testing frequency and criterion for successful testing and how the tests and exercises will be conducted in an effective manner to yield desired results.
- Have the procedure of how the tests and exercises need to be planned and implemented, and clarify post-test/post-exercise follow-up along with ownership of "open items, their owner, and its closure date" as observed during these tests and exercises.
- Have details of how the different management plans are correlated and "how these plans would interact for successfully dealing with a crisis/emergency situation."
- Have details of the dependencies among the plans and also the external dependencies when the different plans *are activated*.

- With a number of "plans in action," there must be clarity in the structure and control of the plans being exercised by a "common owner."
- *Follow a clear hierarchical structure wherein multiple plans come into play during crisis/emergency.*

The management must ensure that the plans and tests are conducted regularly in the right manner with due attention to organization pain points being addressed in the tests and exercises and resulting in a mitigation measure duly incorporated. As there are several plans at the organization level, proper planning must be there to test the validity and currency of all the plans. The aspect of inter-dependence among the plans should be specifically tested so that there are no surprises during any crisis or outage.

Correctly tested plans and exercises bear testimony of the right level of preparedness of its personnel, duly aligned processes being followed during a crisis, and well-aligned technology assisting in smooth conduct of operations that normally are ones that are critical for the organization.

2 ***Close Learnings from Previous Tests and "Gap Closure"*** – Regular and timely tests and exercises give the company and its management a *Reality Check* on the plans' efficacy. These assessments and exercises reveal shortcomings, evidence of the weaknesses and areas of improvement, and potential misalignments with the overall recovery strategy. Tests and exercises can help identify what is working effectively and what is delaying recovery or is incongruent with the overall functioning and synchronization of the various plans. If the tests are done appropriately, the Test Observer, Plan Owner, and Plan Participants can identify plan content that is unattainable, needs reconsideration, needs further alignment to the test/exercise, or can be disregarded due to business conditions. The Business Continuity Planner should follow up on the "open issues" until they are resolved/closed.

Managers and business leaders should view the tests and exercises as a source of improving their resiliency by focusing on the positive effects of these tests and exercises. The positive effects relate to observing the current state of operations, the current way of doing things, and having an open mind to change based on:

a Imminent advantages due to following or not following a current practice.
b A change offered with the advent of technology.
c A change while adopting a "re-engineering solution."
d Adopting a change triggered by its success for the competitor or other industry participant.

e   Adopting the new and upgraded version of technology.

f   Adopting practices that aid in optimal utilization of available limited resources.

g   Adopting a change in operational process that will result in better output and improved performance of the organization.

Operations personnel can also benefit from a critical analysis of the results of the tests and exercises. The points of observation, observers' notes and comments, the contents of test and exercise reports, contents of participants' forms, and the overall conduct of the test/exercise can be good indicators for identifying "gaps" that can add to organization resilience when the change is adopted.

These gaps may relate to the matter pertaining to people practice or to the operational process or in relation to better utilization of technology or the need for upgrades of the solutions pertaining to the current practices in the organization. These may involve re-thinking by the management of such organizations into adopting something new or something that has not been a convention in the organization. Tests and exercises are used as important gap assessment measures to effectively find solutions for anomalies in the current plans and to synchronize the working of different plans. The sync establishes the comprehensiveness of the multiple plans working in a successful manner – serving the different objectives and outcomes of each of the plans.

3   ***Validate Effectiveness of Training and Awareness of BCM*** – Management must also assess resiliency. This means that management should know how well BCM has been ingrained in the mindset of organization personnel, which will guide their actions in a crisis or emergency. As BCM is expensive, an organization should be able to evaluate its effectiveness. The management and its personnel should have some mechanism to understand the current level of BCM proliferation and should know the level of clarity the staff has in matters relating to the understanding and implementation of BCM. Feedback on BCM training and awareness should guide its proliferation. The organization should measure staff's role clarity during a crisis or emergency and whether they know their *Dos and Don'ts* in any situation, including a crisis or emergency. All staff should be aware of what constitutes a crisis and what does not.

This also relates to the point of organization culture. The culture of the organization also plays a pivotal role in the success of anything new being adopted or introduced in the company. As cultures are equally driven by inherent values, it becomes important for the business continuity planner to understand *what works well with the people and what does not.* In organizations with an open culture of positivity for everything that benefits the organization and its personnel, the implementation of BCM may be far easier than in organizations that do not have such an open culture. In organizations with a *not-so-open culture,* the business continuity planner has to consider overcoming this important factor when planning for business continuity implementation. It has been observed that in organizations that have a forward-looking management team that embraces changes in the market and its environment, the culture as *driven from the top* has a very positive impact on the culture in the organization as a whole, and operations in such companies are able to realize the benefits of BCM faster.

4   **Reality Check for "Crisis Readiness"** – *Crisis* readiness reality checks are one of the most crucial tasks for top management. This reality check measures the organization's and its employees' readiness to manage any crisis, disaster, outage, or disruption with minimal downtime. Such organizations may assess any event turning into an "approaching crisis," understand the likely consequences, and undertake necessary steps as per written processes or trigger action for "proper flow of information inputs" for management to make judgments. The organization's preemptive response shields it from the worst of the incident and minimizes its losses.

   Such reality checks during the peace time initiatives also help in building confidence of the personnel, who then are sure of the contents of the plans, their individual roles and responsibilities during the crisis, and their knowledge of the process dependencies – both internal and external, knowledge of "who will lead during crisis, who will decide during crisis and as to the next steps for their operations following the management decision." There are greater chances that any major change in the business environment gets incorporated as updates in the plan and will not come up as a surprise during any actual crisis or emergency. The changed scenario at ground level is better interpreted and understood if the changed circumstances have a financial impact on business continuity readiness and on the organization's crisis response.

5   **Ensure Supply Chain Resiliency, Business Continuity Preparedness of Vendors-Suppliers, Ensuring "Is Our Critical Dependency Covered in Their Plans?"** – The time of BAU is also a time when organizations should validate issues and matters that will have relevance in case of any incident that will require all the management bandwidth for attaining the desired outcomes that protect the interests of the organization, its personnel, its customers, and its stakeholders. It is during this time that management can have peaceful think-through of

all that is required for continuity of its operations. One major component of this thinking is the organization's supply chain resiliency, which primarily relates to having a robust supply chain risk management (SCRM).

During business as usual, organizations should validate issues and matters that will be relevant in the event of an incident that will require all management *bandwidth* to achieve the desired outcomes that protect the interests of the organization, its personnel, its customers, and its stakeholders. Management can peacefully consider all that is needed to maintain operations, including supply chain resiliency, which is mostly related to SCRM.

In commercial terms, a supply chain represents a network of production or service facilities that procures raw materials and transforms them into intermediate or final goods or as a component of service made available to the end customer through an established distribution system. The robustness of the supply chain is critical as any instance of disruption may result in disruption of production or delay in production of the intermediate good or product. This stoppage or delay in operations can have a major impact on the dependent supply chain on any of the following:

a   Delay in meeting customer delivery timeline.
b   Increase in cost of operation or cost of production.
c   Instances of financial liability and penalties on account of breach of contract.
d   Loss of market opportunity.
e   Consequences due to operational re-work and timeline involved.
f   Need for integrating risk management with commodity strategy with suppliers to ensure continuous supply.
g   Need to understand the emerging risks that may impact the supply chain, for example:

  i   Cyber risk.
  ii   Financial risk (covering supplier financial viability and supply market viability).
  iii   Operational risk (covering demand risk, process risk, environmental risk, and operational business continuity planning).
  iv   Understanding supply chain fraud, corruption, and counterfeiting in the supply chain.

From the above, it is evident that these are initiatives that are time consuming and require considerable efforts on the part of the management to come up with clear strategies for countering these risks. The supply chain risk is covered in more detail in the chapter

Supply Chain – The Silent Lifeline for Success of Risk, Crisis, and Business Continuity Management.

6 **Operative Readiness of People, Processes, and Technology. All Critical Applications, Systems, and Equipment to be Working in Line with Their Potential** – Organizations should test their operational readiness to handle crises and disruptions during non-crisis or BAU time. The management of organizations should ensure that such validation exercises of testing the readiness of their personnel to deal with different types of outages, the continuity of operational processing despite hindrance caused by outage, and the ability of technology to support operations and continue operations with certain technology components not supporting due to IT outage are done regularly and on schedule during peace time.

   After identifying its critical operations, resources, technology, and internal and external dependencies during the Business Impact Analysis stage of the business continuity program implementation, the organization can clearly see how to continue its critical operations and business interests, which are vital to its survival. During BAU, management should encourage operations to ensure that alternate plans are in place for important business continuity planning components to avoid any unnecessary or lengthy disruptions. This technique shows management's proactiveness in finding factors that can severely disrupt operations and how the organization has a Plan B to mitigate these risks.

7 **Consider the Current Market Situation, Adopt a Technological Developments-Based Solution, Leverage Upgradation and Improvised Technical Solutions** – BAU is also a time when management teams can analyze dynamic market conditions to adopt any technique or new technology and process that will benefit the corporation in a crisis or disaster. This is a moment when enterprises need to be aware of market trends, competitor actions, and how technology may be used to improve resilience. Management should also comprehend real-time risk assessment and trigger the early warning system for mitigation. Organization staff should know how to incorporate new stuff into their written and authorized documents, as well as the procedure and time required for such approvals.

   Management should develop clear routes for getting the right information during a crisis or emergency to make a quick, deliberate decision that protects the firm and its employees.

8 **Develop Plan B and Plan C in Case of a Long and Extended Outage, Including Operating from Multiple Delivery Centers and Channels** – Upon clear understanding of its critical operations and what it takes to

continue the same during any crisis, emergency, or disruption, management in organizations should be in a position to develop a Plan B or a Plan C to counter a situation of a crisis causing inoperability of Plan A or the primary arrangement for continuity of the critical operations. This kind of exercise will ensure the following purposes are achieved in a meaningful and effective way:

a Clear strategies for known SPOFs (single points of failure).
b Due planning for adopting an alternate solution in case of concentration of risk.
c "Not putting all eggs in the same basket."
d Having approved plans that are alternate to primary ones, in case of any issue with the primary plan.
e Having alternate plans for cost saving in case of dysfunctional Plan A.
f Ensuring that critical operations of the organization do not get hampered and do not result in default and breach of contract, financial liability, penal interest, action by regulator, legal case, adverse media attention, etc.
g Ensuring alternate readiness of people, process, and technology connectivity to protect stakeholder interest.
h Ensuring management and organization personnel have "peace of mind" during any crisis, especially where crisis results in extended outage.
i As a test strategy for trying something new that will result in increasing and improving performance, saving costs, enhancing customer engagement, adopting new and innovative technology, incorporating results of innovation, and exploring new and re-engineering options, etc.
j Having alternate plans in compliance with management diktat or to comply with regulatory requirement as directed by the regulator.

It will be observed that all the above-listed initiatives can be planned, implemented, and executed better for their success when they are deliberated during BAU time without pressure from any quarter for a quick decision or a quick response normally required during any crisis or emergency.

9 *Have a Realistic Strategy for Risk Horizon Scanning* – Management should constantly monitor the risk horizon and prepare a response. It is commonly understood that risks, when handled properly, may safeguard the organization and its personnel, and that any crisis can be an opportunity for the organization if its personnel are ready to capitalize on it. This means that during peace time, management

should evaluate the full scope of a crisis or interruption and how to better prepare for it. For key operations continuity, the Business Continuity Planner should be able to evaluate all business continuity requirements according to BCM Standard. Apart from key activities, the company should foresee and make crisis-related decisions to help itself and its employees. These may involve pre-arrangements with vendors and suppliers for a minimum support and service level during crises based on stricter terms than BAU terms.

To avoid the concentration of dependence on a single power supplier, the corporation used a strategic power supplier to provide "mobile power support through a portable generator unit" to address local hazards and threats. Such strategic arrangements reduce risk and allow the organization to calculate the "cost of this arrangement."

10 **Establish a Connection with Local Authorities and Government Departments/Agencies** – It is a reality that during any crisis or emergency, the organization and its personnel will require help and assistance from various quarters to deal with different situations because of the increased risk and threat scenarios. The management of organizations by their timely, actions, and decisions is expected to protect them from all risks to their reputation, market share, personnel, customers, and stakeholders. It then follows that management teams must be prepared to support their people during crisis, and for this, they must be able to garner support from the right quarters as appropriate in the crisis situation.

The type of emergency will govern what support the management has to render for protecting the organization. It is in this context that management teams are expected to establish and maintain cordial relationships with the civil and civic authorities. These represent the government department and agencies that carry out civic and civil duties on the part of the government. They represent departments such as the electricity supply, water supply, municipality, police and hospital services, emergency responders, etc. It is important for organizations to develop good working relationship with the above-listed authorities as these relationships can be leveraged to solve issues and matters during a crisis or disruption scenario.

Due to heightened risk and hazard scenarios, organizations and their staff will need outside help to handle crises and emergencies. The management of a business must safeguard its reputation, market share, people, customers, and stakeholders by their actions and decisions. Thus, the management team must be ready to support its people in a crisis and be able to get the correct support. Management support for organization protection depends on the type of emergency and management teams must maintain good relations with civil and civic authorities in this setting. These government entities represent utilities, municipalities, police, hospitals, and emergency responders. Organizations need solid working connections that can be leveraged to solve issues and matters during crisis or any disruption scenario. Having a solid working relationship with government agencies is crucial, but so is adding value to each other. Sharing their methods and plans helps civil authorities support the organization amid crises. Since the authorities have contact with all the other players, they can suggest changes and improvisations in the organization's crisis readiness and introduce it to other good practices and ways of handling crisis while effectively using people, processes, and more advanced technology solutions and options to overcome the crisis/emergency. This formal "public-private partnership" has been successful in assisting disaster response and recovery. These partnerships conserve human and inanimate resources (e.g., hardware, software, facilities, technology, etc.).

11   *Develop Key-Strategic Partnerships* – As stated in #10 above, once effective relationships are established, especially with government departments, operations teams and organization personnel can feel more confident in their ability to handle any outage and have better clarity about their individual role and responsibility and the collective ability to handle the crisis/emergency. The organization can establish structured processes for staff to follow defined procedures and plans to ensure continuity of operations and resume critical operations. At this point, managers must build essential ties and strategic partnerships that the firm may use during outages and disruptions. These partnerships give the organization access to information and resources that can help managers make better decisions to protect the organization's interests.

Strategic alliances provide access to professional advice and solutions, which is especially helpful for firms in times of crisis. Experience sharing about the issue might also be used. Sharing past incidents and how they were handled is another method to use such relationships. Information repository/regional forums for experience exchange and "joint preparedness," etc.

12   *Explore Options for Reducing Costs of BCM by Adopting New Solutions for Continuity of Critical Operations* – As mentioned, BCM can help a company find cheaper options and optimize resources during a crisis, ensuring that only the minimum is spent to recover vital processes. Rationalizing organizational resources like people, processes, and technology can also boost robustness. Organization can also explore increasing resiliency through rationalization of organizational resources of people faculties, process upgrades, and technology as an enabler.

13 *Explore Deployment of Best Practices Adopted in the Industry and by "Other Players"* – The organization can benefit from adopting the best practices and utilize the experiences of other *industry players*. This way it can deploy the latest practices for dealing with a crisis/emergency.

Conclusion

From the preceding contents it can be inferred that for crisis and emergency planning, an ideal time is the *BAU* time when all thinking and deliberations about risks and uncertainties need to be addressed objectively. The management can proactively consider the 360 degrees of any untoward situation and prepare structured plans, laying down comprehensive and systematic coordination of organization resources of its people, processes, and enabling technology. BAU is a time that should be used to *plan for the worst* and line up all resources for successful and expeditious recovery from any crisis. There are numerous initiatives that organizations can implement that can be a barometer for organizations' crisis readiness.

Key Take-Aways

- Crisis preparedness should be tested during BAU times and not during the crisis itself. The organization may be a "paper tiger" with untested crisis management plans.
- Clarity of staff for their specific role and responsibility can be crucial for successfully dealing with a crisis/emergency.
- Effectiveness of training and awareness in BCM should be validated regularly.
- Real-world events should guide risk horizon scanning and taking appropriate safeguards.
- Organizations' external dependencies and supply chain risk for critical operation should have a Plan B and a Plan C (alternate strategy in case of any issue with primary strategy).

Chapter 6

Technology Resilience

How Much Should a BC Manager Know and Contribute?

Technology today is the biggest enabler for any organization – large or small. Technology, along with its component of applications, software, hardware, and peripherals, has assumed an integral position in the recovery and resumption of business post any incident or crisis. Just as a doctor needs to know and understand the symptoms before he/she can start any treatment for any ailment, similarly a business continuity manager must know and understand the components and dynamics of the technology and its architecture – to ensure that IT support is well planned for any incident for the IT team to enable the organization to resume its critical part of operations. The business continuity manager must possess the required understanding and leverage the same with the IT manager to ensure that business objectives are attained in a timely manner.

Human thinking has helped apply resources throughout human evolution. Man has thus "evolved" from doing manual tasks to mechanization through machines, with technology improving machine capability with the application of AI, cyber proficiency, cloud computing, robotics, etc. Man has always tried to exploit technology's metamorphic quality to benefit society, at least for civilian purposes. Thus, humans have sought to use technology to accomplish tasks that would otherwise take a long time or a lot of effort. These innovations have helped humans use technology for self-gain and community benefit.

Knowledge fosters the right information and wisdom for the person. When facing a crisis, emergency, or disruption, personnel must act in the best interest of the organization to protect its reputation, its market share, its financial position, the interest of its personnel, and the interest of its other stakeholders. The preparedness to perform the right action and prompt staff to act as per predefined and predesignated roles adds to the resiliency of the organization. The resiliency of the organization gets directly correlated with its capability to deal with a crisis, emergency, or business continuity situation. These three areas will need to be supported by plans for recovery and resumption of operations at the earliest possible

DOI: 10.4324/9781003304678-6

time to ensure that the critical operations are resumed and recovered as soon as possible should there be any outage or disruption.

This chapter will help readers and practitioners comprehend technology, its intricacies, its application, and how it improves operational efficiency for product and service delivery. If technical expertise is lacking or there is a technological outage and end-customer requirements are urgent, it is crucial to comprehend the ramifications. If *Plan A* is interrupted, progressive organizations, management, and managers must have a *Plan B* alternative. Technology failure should not derail the working of the company or its employees. Such outages test the organization's crisis readiness and distinguish it from its competitors.

The above explanation implies that the staff supporting the organization during a crisis, emergency, or operational disruption should be able to assess the *gravity of the situation* and its consequences. This assessment should help company staff understand critical business activities and how long they would take to resume after the outage. The *gravity of the situation* and the enormity of the impact drive the assessment of the incident by the EMT (Emergency Management Team), CMT (Crisis Management Team), BCM (Business Continuity Management) team, and/or the IT DRT (IT Disaster Recovery Team). Crisis and emergency procedures guide this assessment, and the management approves these documented procedures.

The BCM team and CMT must thus understand the *real situation, its impact to its operations, and the time it would take to resume operations, at least the critical part.* It is for this reason it becomes imperative for the Business Continuity Manager to have a BASIC MINIMUM UNDERSTANDING OF TECHNOLOGY AND ITS APPLICATION. He/she should understand how technology is organized in the company, what is its basic configuration, what is its high-level architecture, what is its detailing around hardware and software application, and what are key IT assets and their relevance in running the critical operations of the company. The above are only some of the examples, though not exhaustive, about technology and how its knowledge will help business continuity manager in contributing to critical business recovery.

Let us consider this specific point in more detail and see how the BCM team and its manager can perform their role and responsibility in an effective manner when:

- *"They Have Knowledge of Technology That Helps Them Understand the Bigger Picture"* – The BCM team/manager understands the overall impact of any outage and can anticipate what could go wrong and how they should prepare themselves to deal with the situation.

- *They Can Give a Better Solution* – After understanding the outage's impact, the business continuity manager can propose a solution that best serves the organization and optimizes resources.
- *They Understand the "Real Issue and Its Real Impact"* – The business continuity manager can identify the root cause of the outage by understanding IT, technology, configuration, and architecture.
- *They Understand the Flow of the Transaction Life Cycle* – With sufficient knowledge of deployed technology and *what is happening and what will be the outcome and how the situation can be controlled by a timely action.* After understanding operations process technicalities, the BCM team/manager can initiate early action.
- *They Understand the Dependencies, Their Nature, the Resources Required, and the Downside if Operations Are Not Supported* – The BCM team/manager may need internal and external help to handle outages and crises. They need active support for crisis situations where they are uniquely dependent on others. To contribute effectively during *crunch time* dependencies must be pre-identified, and all *parties* must know their roles.
- *They Would Know the five Ws and one H during Any Technology Outage* – The BCM team/manager would know the critical details of how technology affects business operations. The team analyzes the crisis's five Ws – What, Where, When, Who, Why – and one H-How, to resonate with a better solution and response.
- *In the Unfortunate Event of an Accident, They Understand the Nature and Extent of Damage and What It Would Take to Restore Operations and the Related Timeline* – *The* BCM team/manager is better prepared to handle crises and outages if they understand the technology and its capabilities. They know what happened, how, when, where, and who is responsible for its recovery. Understanding and segregation aid objective crisis response, limiting damage and protecting stakeholder interests.
- *They Understand How the Technology Architecture Is Organized* – The business continuity manager "knows the technology components" with a basic understanding of technology architecture. This knowledge helps employees understand the company's technology map, which links hardware and software. They understand the *ripple effect of any technology going wrong.*
- *The BCM Standards Require Continual Improvement* – The BCM team/manager always endeavors to maintain and improve the BCM implementation by following the BCP policy and implementation as per governance framework, adequate training, and awareness of internal and external parties, etc. The organization personnel will be able to do better proliferation upon understanding the nitty-gritty aspect of the enabling technology.

- **They Understand the Importance and Relevance of IT and OT Systems –**
IT and OT systems are the main services of the IT Department.
Understanding each system's function and organizational purpose
enables user–technology synergy. IT systems enable user–technology
synergy by connecting users to technological applications. The back-end
OT system makes IT systems run smoothly. IT issues can be fixed by the
local IT team, but OT issues, unless minor, require the OEM (Original
Equipment Manufacturer). If the BCM team/manager can understand
the technology issue, its impact, and the likely time to restore connectivity or fix the "IT issue," they can greatly benefit the business during a
crisis or disruption.
- **They Can Establish Better Connect Using a "Partnership Approach"
for Supporting the Business Unit (BU) with due Assistance from IT –**
After understanding BU issues and operations, the BCM team/manager
would have a better relationship with the IT team. They can work
together during crises with a *partner* approach. The BCM team/manager
can use their IT connections to find the best solution to help the
organization recover. To protect the organization and its stakeholders,
all employees work together. However, such programs should be
organized during *peace time and not during crisis or war time.*
- **Result in Better Planning and Coordination between BU and IT with
due Facilitation from the BCM Team/Manager –** Upon understanding
the operations of the BUs and their requirement for continuing critical
business, the BCM team/manager can arrive at a better continuity
solution based on IT and technology required for continuity. Adequate
understanding of IT/technology helps a better coordination between
the BU and IT as the BCM team/manager can "make the demand meet
the supply."
- **They Can Help Management Make Right and Timely Decisions during
Crisis/Disruption –** By understanding the *technology set-up* in the
organization, the BCM team/manager can better assess the impact and
consequences of any disruption and the expected time to resume IT
asset use, network and connectivity, or service. The BCM team inputs to
the BCM Steering Committee or senior management can help *assess
the real ground situation* and make an informed decision. Thus, BUs,
management, the BCM team/manager, and supporting BUs can remain
calm during crises and focus on value-creating activities and resuming
critical operations.
- **They Can "Broker the Exact Business Requirement" between the BU
and the IT/Technology Team –** After the business impact analysis and
risk assessment, the BCM team/manager creates the BU's Business
Continuity Plan. They know how important BU operations are. The
BCM team/manager helps both the BU and the IT-technology team by

clarifying the BU's critical operations continuity requirements during disruptions or outages.

- **They Can Be the Bridge between the User and the IT/Technology Team** – The IT/technology team must maintain adequate security "controls and patches" that are deployed from time to time to prevent hacking, phishing, network outages, security breaches, etc. Some protocols take hours to complete. The BCM team/manager can help plan the proposed IT upgrade without disrupting business operations or BUs by understanding technology and IT upgrades. When done during non-working hours or low-volume operations, such initiatives can reduce lost productive man-hours. IT actions should be done during "peace time" rather than emergencies.

BUs and the BCM team/managers must also consider existing and emerging risk scenarios that could impact any enterprise or organization's business operations. These dangers are real and could strike at any time due to natural or human causes, and the organization staff must be prepared during *peace time* to face these risks and threats. This resilience relates to the organization's ability to recover from adversities and untoward incidents and is commonly associated with risk identification, its appropriate treatment, and identification of single point of failures. Replication and redundancy controls *plug* these exposures. Risk analysis must quantify these risks and threats to address and manage them. Treatment quantifies risk.

In the parlance of the BCM Standards, the risk assessment involves the activities of:

- Identification of risk.
- Assessing its likelihood and impact.
- Recommending mitigation measures and preparing product/service risk and its impact matrix followed by implementing risk controls.

While the list of possible risks can be quite long, the main categories relate to the following:

- Natural Disasters.
- Health and Human Resource Related Issues.
- Operational and Man-Made Disasters.
- Equipment and Supply Failures.
- Business and Compliance Related Risks.
- External and Financial Risks.
- Risk of Fraud and Claims.
- Technology and Infrastructure Failure.

Let us now discuss *technology and infrastructure failure* like technology risks due to infra set-up, cloud solution, cyber threat, hardware or software failure, network and power failure, operator error, or premature technology obsolescence. The BCM team/manager must understand these risks to determine the cause and timeline of the disruption to critical business operations. They can advise BUs in a systematic, structured, and timely manner based on available information about human and cultural factors enabled by technology and systems.

Business continuity managers must understand basic technology infrastructure and high-level architecture. They can then understand the role and function of the enabling technology and its capability in network connectivity, response time, security features deployed, IT assets deployed, and the IT asset role in the organization. The BCM team/manager should use a transaction workflow from user login to audit review to understand technology setup. Let us examine the following pointers to help you understand how concepts in technology deployment and applications can be effectively used for enhancing organizational resilience:

A   Basics of IT Network Connectivity, its Architecture, and Configuration

A good understanding of the technology will enable the BCM team/manager to understand intricacies of the network, its connectivity and firewalls, and routing to and role of servers with *load balancing*. It is noteworthy to know the role of switches, routers, load balancers, racks, and blades, which are critical for "IT performance." All the knowledge can help for an optimized IT strategy for quick recovery.

B   IT Systems and OT Systems

Normally the IT Channels comprise (a) Online Services, (b) Mobile Applications, (c) Third-Party Applications, (d) Core Systems, and (e) Supporting Systems. The supporting systems then get bifurcated into business support – the IT systems for the organization and the IT support system – the OT systems for the organization (operating systems).

Information Technology (IT) is responsible for the control of an organization's data, whereas Operational Technology (OT) oversees the actual operations. IT can be used to make OT systems easier to operate by monitoring them for issues, and giving real-time status reports. Segregation of IT and OT systems along with recovery time objective (RTO) and recovery point objective (RPO) will ensure clarity on IT recovery and a timeline based on the nature of the outage.

The BCM team/manager should add value to boost operational efficiency and production at any industrial manufacturing enterprise, impacting overall process efficiency and ensuring sustainability through predictive analytics and data science, guiding recovery efforts toward achieving organization objectives of cost savings, performance enhancement, improved flexibility, compliance to security protocols, and operational standards.

C Cyber Security Risk

Cyber security risk relates to the loss of data, information, and information control systems that may directly impact or have the potential to adversely impact the organization's operations, thereby having a negative impact on its image or reputation, organization assets, and individuals. The prime reason for this risk is the compromise of CIA (confidentiality, integrity, availability) of the above-listed factors. A typical example of cyber risk is the risk of system sabotage or data theft by internal or external parties. When a cyber-attack is perpetrated, it is normally done with the malicious intention of gaining access to information, financial gain, espionage, or sabotage. It is a deliberate act for unauthorized breaches in security to gain access to security systems.

The cyber risks due to acts of internal employees can be monitored and guided in the long run by adequate training and awareness to users on the relevance of *security patches and timely upgrades of software and applications*. The BCM team/manager should ensure that the users are made aware of the consequences of their *IT behavior* and the protection of the organization's IT interest.

The key steps for enhancing cyber security resilience are as follows:

- *Secure the organization's* network from attacks by deploying security controls and filtering for unauthorized access.
- *Educate users* about the impending risks posed by cyber risks and threats.
- *Prevent malware* by preparing policies and procedures.
- *Control removable media.*
- *Configure the security* by implementing security patches.
- *Monitor as a strategy* to ensure that systems are monitored nonstop and that the data and logs are appropriately analyzed for appropriate action to be initiated in the event of any kind of cyber-attack.
- Create and develop *incident management plans* based on foreseeable risks, and test the plan for its effectiveness.
- *Manage and monitor user privileges* to ensure that all system rights and accesses are in line with the job role.
- Establish the *"risk management culture"* based on evaluation of possible and potential risks and threats to the technology and information systems, and embed an appropriate risk management culture across the organization.

Cyber Defense

It is a reality that cyber criminals are ever-active and continue to innovate and evolve their attack and phishing techniques. Organizations and their business continuity teams need to be specifically aware of the risk of ransom attacks on the IT assets of the company. The attackers are constantly using new and smarter ways of attacking, causing greater damage, and these increased stakes increase the amounts of ransom as well. While the organization cannot predict these attacks, it is prudent for their BCM team/manager to at least be prepared to face the risk, minimize its damage, and deal with "ransom issue" appropriately. It is for this reason that the BCM team/manager should take measures before, during, and after the attack so that there is minimal damage to the brand and reputation, market share, financials, and stakeholders. The three stages of actions are covered in the section as follows:

Cyber Defense: Before, During, and After a Ransomware Attack

Andy Stone, in his article "A 3-Step Approach to Cyber Defense: Before, During & After a Ransomware Attack," has covered this aspect very effectively in suggesting the following three-step approach:

Before: Beware during Business as Usual – The organization should practice IT hygiene with documented procedures, have multi-factor authentication to address the risk of weak passwords and related vulnerabilities, practice admin credential vaulting of access to systems, and have fast real-time analytics to identify suspicious behavior with timely alerts on potential attacks and critical employee training.

During: As the Attack Unfolds – The IT team should put the backup communication plan into action, mobilize the ERT, initiate the external communication plan, and start the forensic process to identify what type of attack was launched and its severity. The sooner the team ascertains, the sooner it can apply patches as safeguards.

After: Steps to Recovery – Organization management should respond to the attack with speed and quick decisions, prioritize the recovery of systems, including addressing the dependencies, and communicate progress to impacted parties and other stakeholders (employees, customers, investors, partners, suppliers, service providers, etc.), work with and inform regulators in a timely manner, work offline to identify and eradicate any persistent malware infections, deploy alternate production devices for those that are not fit for reuse, and stage a recovery environment and test it to get back online asap.

In an unfortunate event of a cyber-attack, the BCM team/manager should be able to discern the type of attack while collaborating with IT.

D   Cloud Computing

With the advancement in technology and the extreme pressure on cost and profit margins for organizations, it is critical for the BCM team/manager to understand and keep pace with the development and innovative solutions that technology offers and how these are useful for the overall organization. The knowledge of cloud computing and its detailing around its architecture, design, and deployment models across different organizations can help the BCM team/manager come up with more economical and competent business continuity solutions.

The concept of *cloud computing* refers to the delivery of information technology-related services via the Internet. Cloud computing enables enterprises to have access to adaptable information technology solutions that are founded on transparent service agreements. Cloud computing is a model that enables ubiquitous, convenient, and on-demand network access to a shared pool of configurable computing resources (e.g., networks, servers, storage, applications, and services).

These resources can be rapidly provisioned and released with minimal management effort or interaction from service providers. In academia, the term "cloud computing" refers to a model that enables this. For example, a cloud computing model would enable on-demand network access to a shared pool of configurable computing resources. This model of cloud computing is made up of a total of seven basic qualities, three service types, and four deployment models, as detailed in Table 6.1 hereunder:

Table 6.1 Cloud Computing Model – Characteristics, Features, and Deployment

7 Essential Characteristics	3 Service Types	4 Deployment Models
• On-demand self service • Broad network access • Multi-tenancy & resource pooling • Rapid elasticity & scalability • Pay-per-use • Multi-tenancy • Measured service	• SaaS: Software as a Service - *Business Application Users* • PaaS: Platform as a Service - *Platform & Middleware for Application developers* • IaaS: Infrastructure as a Service - *Computing power, storage & other IT infrastructure*	• Public cloud • Private cloud • Community cloud, & • Hybrid cloud

The BCM team/manager, with a little more effort, can understand the typical examples of each of the services. This will help them understand the hosting of applications and services on the cloud and ease of access during any crisis or disruption. They will be able to relate to the critical services being hosted on the cloud and the options available for their recovery and the related timelines. This knowledge will also help in validating the results of the Business Impact Analysis and whether the RTO/RPOs are realistic and achievable.

In the overall interest of organization resiliency duly enhanced by effective implementation of business continuity, the BCM team/manager should develop a detailed understanding of the nitty-gritties of the cloud characteristics, its service types, and its deployment models. This will also help them in advising BUs with respect to cost-saving BCM solutions and optimization of resources in "crunch time" or during a crisis. Some of the important concepts and terms that the BCM team/manager should be familiar with are as follows:

1   Application hosting.
2   License cost/pay per use.
3   Multi-tenancy.
4   Web-based interfaces.
5   Emulation.
6   Hosted service & web-based interfaces.
7   Physical and virtual server.
8   Storage space.
9   Network connection & its topologies (star, point-to-point, bus, ring or circular, mesh, tree, hybrid, etc.).
10   IP addresses.
11   Routers and load balancers.
12   Bandwidth.
13   Virtualization.
14   Managed services.
15   Cloud architecture (multi-purpose, multi-tenancy, or service-oriented).

The BCM team/manager upon understanding the above concepts, apart from adding to the resiliency of the organization, can also provide additional benefits by effectively understanding the concepts of cloud computing to be utilized in developing realistic and SMART recovery objectives, such as:

1   Reduced cost.
2   Speed and time-to-market.
3   Emerging technologies.
4   Automation.
5   Flexibility in operating models.
6   Shared resources.
7   Agility and scalability.
8   More IT functionality for a lower price.

E Critical Security Controls

BU managers must know what assets to protect, what is the output of the BIA in the business continuity management program, and what should be done to protect and continue critical operations using security controls. The result is the need and requirement for the critical role of security monitoring, incident response in case something happens, and an adequate system backup to fall back on and make recovery possible. The critical data and information about operations are known, and the same gets protected as part of the critical internal security control.

The BCM team/manager along with IT must constantly endeavor to identify unprotected IT assets that are vulnerable to attack, and any new asset installed must adhere to the pre-installation checks, controls, and security configured and patched as per requirement. Also, the BCM team/ manager along with IT must identify *non-critical systems* that are vulnerable and can be used by attackers to penetrate the network and systems. The IT must have knowledge and documentation relating to *weak security configuration* so that the appropriate controls on them shall ensure that they "do not aid the attackers." The BCM team/manager must be aware of the business IT assets that are used for demonstration purposes, testing purposes, and as *guest machines*. These should be isolated from the network to prevent unauthorized access affecting the security of enterprise operations.

From the above, it can be inferred that all IT systems in the network, whether critical or non-critical, need to be monitored (in differential degree of relevance) and that all portable end-user devices, especially with so many staff WFH (working from home) post Covid and because of post Covid cost initiatives where these devices *touch the network temporarily* because they can be used by attackers to penetrate network systems. These assets also need to be actively monitored.

It may be prudent for the BCM team/manager to collaborate with IT to assess the needs and requirements of appropriate security controls in line with the nature and complexity of business operations, expanse of IT assets, complexity of IT architecture, and configuration and applications and software deployed for security controls. The BCM team may cover some or all the following areas for security controls and possess adequate knowledge regarding:

- Inventory & Control of Enterprise Assets & Software Assets.
- Data Protection.
- Configuration of Enterprise Assets & Software Assets.
- Access Control Management.
- Audit Log Management.
- Email & Web Browser Protection.
- Malware Defenses.

- Data Protection & Data Recovery.
- Network Infrastructure Management.
- Security Awareness & Skills Training.
- Service Provider Management.
- Application Software Security.
- Incident Response Management.
- Penetration Testing.

As an abundant caution to the BCM team/manager, they must collaborate with the BU and the IT team, to assist and support the IT team in doing their primary function. At no point in time should it be deemed that the BCM team is supplementing the role of the organization's IT, and the involvement is only from a standpoint of defining and deciding with respect to RTOs and the ability of BUs to meet the defined RTO.

Conclusion

This brings us to the end of this chapter. For the closing note, it would be an understatement that the knowledge of technology and its application can help the BCM team/managers, business continuity champions in BU's, and the BCM Steering Committee to understand the full impact of technology, its prowess, its weaknesses, and its fallacies.

In the preceding pages, we have seen how the BCM team/manager can perform their role and responsibility in an effective manner by assisting the BUs and their managers in all phases of the BCM life cycle and how they can assist in doing meaningful business impact analysis, conduct risk and threat assessment, and formulate BCPs for its critical operations while also addressing the need for strategic alliance and partnership with key stakeholders relevant for the continuity of critical business.

It has been explained how a basic knowledge of technology, its architecture, its configuration, and its components can be utilized by the BCM team/manager in understanding the *technology-related aspect of business operations* and how this understanding can be used in formulating a continuity strategy while validating the RTOs and RPOs and that breaching of these would result in negative consequences for the organization.

We've also seen how the BCM team/manager can help BUs respond to cyber-attacks by using their technology knowledge. Preparation before, during, and after a cyber-attack can reduce the damage to organization assets, both physical and otherwise. A peek into the techniques deployed by hackers will help readers to understand the various attack modes hackers deploy for cyber-attacks.

There is increased pressure on organizations for profitability, and executive teams are struggling to find ways and means to impact top-line growth and cut bottom-line costs. In doing so, executive management is considering multiple options involving rationalization of people, processes, and technology. On the technology aspect, IT is exploring the cloud offering by various providers. The cloud, with its characteristics, its types of services, and its deployment models, which have been covered at a high level, along with the detailing of technology and the benefits of adopting cloud technology.

The significance of the critical internal security controls has been covered to explain what the IT, BU personnel, and BCM team/manager must consider while deciding, defining, and designing the IT infrastructure and implementing effective security controls. The relevance of building security in the culture of the organization can be seen as an important pursuit for senior management and how the culture change must be brought about.

Key Take-Aways

- Organization personnel need to understand "What is its technology capable of?"
- Organization personnel should know how to deal with a crisis or emergency and how the technology can be utilized for the solution.
- All organization managements and their managers must anticipate a solution of *Plan B* if the primary *Plan A* is disrupted for any reason.
- The organization must follow a comprehensive approach when activating its EMT, CMT, BCM team, and IT DRT.
- Skills, experience, and expertise of BCM personnel should be leveraged for developing a continuity strategy.
- The cloud option for technology and data should be adopted ONLY AFTER DUE CONSIDERATION of it addressing the IT and security needs.
- Organization management must ensure that it is part of vendor/service providers' crisis response and emergency support in the event of a crisis or emergency.

Chapter 7

Implementing Business Continuity in Oil, Gas, and Energy

Challenges and Issues

Complexity of the production process and supply chain in oil, gas, and energy, along with complexity in operations add to a very high cost of Plan B for business continuity in the oil and gas sector. The culture and diversity in the workforce require a high level of coordination and collaboration. The oil and gas companies' unique issues and challenges add to the practicality of implementing business continuity in an effective manner. The numerous parties in the O&G sector operations add to the need for considering 360 degrees before going in for any specific strategy or solution. This chapter is a case study illustration for this critical industry sector.

The events of the last few decades have amplified the risks and threats scenario for all the denizens of earth and across corporate sectors around the globe. These risks have far-reaching ramifications for organizations, sectors, industries, economies, and countries in such a manner that becomes imperative for the risks and threats to be analyzed to ensure that functions and operation of corporates and organizations continue in a systematic manner. It is important to mention that the same risk and threat may impact the organizations differently, while the organizations may be in the same location, same country, or same sector and be in the same industry. This is primarily due to the inherent nature of risk and individual capacity of organizations that can withstand the risks. Equally important are the unique requirements of these organizations based on their product and service portfolio. Something that may be fine in one organization in one sector by way of risk may be totally unacceptable in another organization. The need and requirement of stakeholders in these organizations may be entirely different while the organizations may have some common factors.

In this chapter, we will be discussing the specific aspect of the challenges and issues while implementing business continuity in any organization in the oil, gas, and energy sector. The extent and expanse of operations in oil, gas, and energy are very extensive and diverse, and this leads to many factors that need to be addressed, especially when implementing business

DOI: 10.4324/9781003304678-7

continuity in these organizations. Oil, gas, and energy as a sector have critical value in all countries as the sector supports the requirements of domestic demand and obligations of commercial and industrial demand across the communities.

The extensive and complex production life cycle in the oil, gas, and energy sector makes it relevant for organization managements to think through for having plans, strategies, and means to mitigate the risks and threats by adopting strategies that will build organization resilience. This is done by establishing CMP (Crisis Management Plan), IMP (Incident Management Plan), ERP (Emergency Response Plan), IT DR (IT Disaster Recovery Plan), BCP (Business Continuity Plan), and MRP (Media Response Plan). It is quite prevalent that these various plans are the responsibility of different personnel in the organization who may belong to different business and support departments. It is this *distributed ownership* of these plans that causes the organization to have *continuity issues* in case of any disruption, and the respective managements must ensure that all these plans function in unison during any crisis or emergency. The plans with different *owners* are *like different drivers all having control of the steering wheel and driving the same organization; however, each is trying to move in their own direction.* It is seldom that the direction is the same in the organization. If *management bonding* is not there, then the direction is also not the same and will cause incongruence in the functioning of such an organization. These organizations conduct themselves with half-hearted efforts based on knee-jerk reactions during crisis and emergency.

To cover this complexity of the oil, gas, and energy production and supply chain aspect, let us consider the natural life cycle of oil and gas from the stage of crude oil to its end products used by the customers as finished oil and gas products.

We will adopt the approach of upstream, middle-stream, then downstream.

Upstream

The upstream segment of oil and gas production refers to the phase consisting of exploration comprising geological surveys and securing legal rights to explore and produce oil and gas through onshore or offshore drilling processes. Oil and gas companies conduct upstream operations based on certain key factors that include the following:

1   Profitability of the oil and gas field in the long run.
2   Number of *producing* wells to be drilled directly impacts the costs and infrastructure attached and thereby the commercial viability.

3   Expected production profile of the field to forecast the annual production volumes from the start of production until the abandonment of the oil well/oil field.

The operations in the life cycle of oil and gas comprise well site selection and its preparation, well drilling, hydraulic fracturing, construction of infrastructure such as the laying down of pipelines and construction of a storage facility, followed by extraction of oil and gas as the natural production activity. From the above, it can be inferred that at the start of upstream phase of oil and gas production, the companies have a very limited scope for implementing business continuity management (BCM) as the activities are driven by pure financial and commercial viability. As BCM considers the establishment of Plan B for the primary operation, should it get disrupted, the same is applicable in a very limited manner and may only address alternate resources being available for the activities listed above.

Now let us also consider the case where upstream operations of the oil and gas are being conducted by the company as a core activity and operations of such companies are also referred to as E&P, the acronym for *exploration and production*. The "explore" in this context refers to oil, natural gas, and condensate. For such companies, the oil and gas life cycle is normal and involves day-to-day oil extraction from the oil well. The nature and complexity of the upstream operations in oil and gas leave very little options for implementing BCM in its true sense following the BCM life cycle. The dynamics of rig operations also get complicated due to its location, be it on land or in the sea. The nature of upstream operations makes it imperative for the management to consider many factors, as listed below, that impede and hamper full-fledged implementation of BCM:

1   *Single Point of Failures (SPOFs) in Upstream Operations* – There are multiple points of failures in upstream operations, which makes it very difficult to build a continuity strategy, and due to the nature of operations, also building risk mitigation plans for upstream operations is a very costly option that negates the very initiative.
2   *Cost of Maintenance & Predictive Maintenance* – As the operations of upstream for oil and gas are quite complex, an approach of maintaining spare equipment may not justify its utility. The costs are so high that the corresponding benefit may not be prudent since the activity involves sophisticated equipment backed by high-end technology to perform the analytics. As the outcome of drilling operations may vary due to physical and other environmental factors, it is equally relevant that organizations have limited options for performing predictive maintenance.
3   *Cost of Equipment and Spares* – Another limiting factor for establishing business continuity in upstream operations is the high cost of equipment

and spares that are required to be put up in the oil field prior to the start of production. There is a lot of planning involved prior to establishing any oil well.

4   **Defining Recovery Time Objective (RTO)** – RTO is the time period after any outage or disruption within which the operations and activities need to restart and resume. In case of upstream operations in oil and gas, determining RTO based on certain pre-conditioned factors is possible; however, there may be indefinite delay due to outage or emergency caused by factors beyond the control of the operations personnel. An example can be an issue with some third-party application or software or a breakdown of equipment having external dependency for repair and maintenance.

5   **Defining Minimum Business Continuity Objective (MBCO)** – The term MBCO refers to the minimum level of services and/or products that is acceptable to the organization for its customers for the organization to achieve its business objectives during an incident, emergency, or disaster. As the operations and output of upstream oil and gas operations are dependent on many factors, it is improbable to arrive at MBCO for upstream business. While the upstream company may define a minimum level of daily production, the level may or may not get achieved due to the factors stated above, and practicing business continuity by its concept can be a challenge. The cost of providing a business continuity solution may not be prudent.

6   **Availability of Skilled Staff** – The upstream oil and gas operations, whether on an oil rig in sea or on land, requires variously qualified personnel. The personnel comprises scientists, geologists, drillers, deck personnel, rig operators, mechanics, medical and safety personnel, cooks, and other support staff, etc. The skills, experience, and educational qualifications for their various positions are different, and organizations maintain appropriate levels of workforce to ensure support to and conduct of its critical business operations.

7   **Health, Safety and Environment Factors** – Safety of personnel and that of assets is a prime concern for managements of upstream oil and gas companies. As the risks and threats faced by both people and assets are high, the remediation cost is equally high. Insurance costs for both categories are very high due to the inherent risks due to fire hazards, climate extremities, and natural hazards. Since these risks cannot be mitigated in absolute terms, the managements must accept and tolerate these risks and need to practice a balanced approach for the risk exposure after mitigation measures and their related cost.

Another important factor to be considered is the amount of *medical readiness* and *medical equipment* along with availability of *medical personnel* at the upstream location. There are very limited options available for addressing the safety aspect, especially for humans, and it is a normal practice to have a mode of air *ambulance* or accessibility to near-shore hospital and medical facility as the business continuity options that can be explored; however, these arrangements need to be tested regularly for their effectiveness. Although assets are insured, the staff must be made aware of their proper usage and follow the right protocol so that the asset is free from accident and mishandling.

8   *Covid and Pandemic Risk* **–** The events of the last three years have highlighted the vulnerability of mankind in dealing with pandemics, and a good number of organizations worldwide have suffered from losses: Loss of life, lost sales, lost business, loss of jobs, period of no or negative growth, loss of confidence, etc.

COVID-19 has been a rude eye-opener in terms of an organization's ability to deal with pandemic impact and how it affected the organization's personnel and disrupted normal operations. With time, humans have adopted counter-measures and adapted their actions to deal with this risk. For the management of upstream oil and gas companies, the pandemic risk is now dealt with in a manner similar to other risk factors, although the solution of social distancing, provision of quarantine, and physical separation are issues that have been addressed at a considerable cost. Due to the nature of upstream operations, these have to be accepted as *co-existing risks, and its cost is unlikely to be defrayed or reduced.*

9   *Nature of Products* **–** The product profile of an upstream oil and gas operation may be crude or its derivative or natural gas. The physical property of crude oil makes it necessary for the oil to be dealt with in a specific and safe manner. These properties are as follows:

a   Topping – loss of extreme volatility due to evaporation.
b   Density/gravity – major value determinant.
c   Pour point – lowest flow temperature before its conversion to solid.
d   Viscosity – characteristic for pipeline flow.
e   Wax content – assessment of wax content in flow pipelines.

It is due to the above physical characteristics of the upstream operations output and the other critical factors listed from 1 to 9 that make it an extremely unlikely case for implementing BCM.

Middle Stream

Middle stream, or midstream as it is more commonly known, is an important phase in the oil and gas industry that serves as an intermediate phase between the upstream and downstream sectors for the purpose of processing, storing, and distributing crude oil, natural gas, and other energy products. This, in turn, means that the midstream phase is characterized by planning logistics, transport of raw materials, infrastructure at the end point for processing, and storage.

To elaborate, the midstream sector covers the transportation, storage, and trading of crude oil, natural gas, and refined products. In its unrefined state, crude oil is transported by these primary modes: Barges, tankers, over land, pipelines, trucks, and railroads for crude oil and through pipelines and liquefied natural gas (LNG) tankers for natural gas.

These transport modes have important aspects to be accounted for, for ensuring the continuity of supply of crude, natural gas, and its derivatives at the refinery or the *processing point* facility. A considered BCM approach will need to be adopted to address some of the issues listed here:

- Truck and pipeline capacity.
- Safety of inventory and personnel during transit.
- Insurance of inventory in transit.
- Safety hazards due to inherent properties of inventory.
- Pipeline maintenance, temperature protocol, pipeline life, etc.
- Under the sea pipeline condition, maintenance, and repair.
- Issues of pollution and spillage with its toxicity impact on human and animal life.

An important aspect that must be borne in mind by a business continuity planner during the midstream phase is the valuation and insurable value of assets, inventory value, and *business value loss* during the handling of product and gas.

The *asset* refers to the physical infrastructure involved in the storage of the product, e.g., oil and gas tanks, etc., and all assets used in logistics and transport. It is crucial that apart from the primary asset covered under *Plan A* for continuity and resilience for the logistics and transport of oil, its derivatives, and gas, the organization must have a *Plan B*, if for any reason the primary asset is unable to perform the transfer of the product, oil, and gas through the bridger trucks, pipeline, railroad, or any other means of transport.

The inventory value refers to the financial valuation of the oil, condensate, chemicals, gas, etc., and their commercial value that governs the contract and sale/purchase agreement terms. As the financial and commercial value are dependent primarily on the demand and supply of crude oil, petroleum, gas, condensate, etc., as determined in the global market, the price is also impacted by other factors such as product quality and its physical attributes. For academic interest, let me explain the valuation of crude oil (brent), and we can use the same mathematical basis for valuing other products.

Oil Price

As the price of oil is market dependent, it becomes extremely difficult for a business continuity planner to judge a particular level of oil price, as the same is fluctuating in line with international trading hours in the oil and gas global market price. As the inventory of crude oil, petroleum, oil, and gas is varying based on production levels/supply and customer demand, the task for a business continuity planner is very tedious in arriving at a minimum inventory value that needs to be considered for continuity of supply, and the BCM planner must also understand the dynamics of the oil price *mathematics*. A basic understanding of this is essential, and accordingly, the oil price should be understood. It is common knowledge that 1 barrel = 42 gallons = 158.98 liters. Suppose oil (brent) price per 1 gallon is USD 2.00/gallon, then, the price of oil (brent) would be USD 84 per barrel or USD 0.5283 per liter.

While the above complexities are there, the BCM planner needs to have some estimate for the base minimum value of the stocks to assist the organization's finance team to leverage this risk against an insurance cover. The BCM planner would then need to ensure implementing controls and facilitate the implementation of operational practices that reduce risks, mitigate the risks, and help the organization have a *Plan B* to counter these risks.

Downstream

Downstream operations in the oil and gas sector represent the phase from post-production to the point of sale. It is the final step of the production process wherein the petroleum, crude oil, condensate, and natural gas are processed to be used by end-user and consumer as usable products. The downstream segment of the petroleum industry mainly comprises three activities: The function of refining oil, manufacture of petrochemicals, and marketing and distribution of refined oil products and natural gas.

The downstream operations in oil and gas involve the recovery and purification of biochemical products through the utilization of the appropriate processing steps. A key starting process in the production life cycle begins in the refinery, where a sequence of processes includes cell separation, filtration, product recovery, extraction of product and purification, and then treatment of product using chemical, physical, and biological means. The products based on their *hydrocarbon* content get separated as different petroleum, oil, and gas products.

Briefly explaining the life cycle of oil will help us in understanding the important part of the life cycle, which may have relevance in the business continuity and factors that should be considered in downstream operations. These high-level steps are segregated as *"core processes"* and *"auxiliary processes"* of refinery operations.

The core processes comprise (a) distillation, (b) cracking, (c) reforming, (d) blending, and (e) treating, and auxiliary processes comprise (a) utilities, (b) power operation, (c) IT and information systems, (d) water & wastewater management, and (e) trading operations.

The subject matter of refinery operations is very vast and is not the scope of our discussion; however, we will be considering the aspect purely from the relevance of business continuity and crisis management. The "refining process" is fraught with complexities from both perspectives, from the perspective of the nature of the product being processed and the infrastructure required for its refining, i.e., the equipment and machinery required to perform the specific process in its refining. The process is explained at a high level to appreciate and understand the specific minimum requirements for business continuity in the core processes and in the auxiliary processes:

1 **Receipt of Desalted Crude Oil or Condensate for Processing –** Condensate is a mixture of light liquid hydrocarbons, like a very light crude oil. It is typically separated out of a natural gas stream at the point of production (field separation) when the temperature and pressure of the gas are dropped to atmospheric conditions.

Distillation – the Physical Separation

2 **The Product Is Put through the Furnace in the "Distillation Tower" in the Refinery –** The process involves heating and vaporization. The effect of heating is that the products get separated as per their boiling points, and the heating is followed by *fractional distillation* – this is done by operating at high atmospheric pressure. The products that get produced are as follows: LPG, gasoline, naphtha, kerosene, jet fuel, diesel, etc.

It is important for the organization to adhere to the regulatory specifications with respect to the production processes and adhere to the environmental control aspect of the production.

Reforming, Blending, and Treating

3 **The Result of #2 Is Also That Products of "Light Cuts" and "Heavy Cuts" Get Separated –** They are called "cuts" because they are the result of separating the crude oil into its constituent parts based on the different temperatures at which they evaporate and condense. The lighter cuts are subjected to chemical reaction to convert the light cuts into other petrochemical products that have industrial and commercial value.

Reforming is a process that is designed to increase the amount of gasoline that can be produced from crude oil. This is accomplished by heating the crude oil to a higher temperature. Based on the inherent hydrocarbon levels, the products get separated.

Blending in a refinery operation refers to blending of different components of crude and gasoline to produce petrochemical products of industrial and commercial value.

Treating in oil and gas refers to the step-in refining process that removes the contaminants and impurities that are normally a natural part of the crude, condensate, or gas. The treatment may comprise reforming and cracking of the crude oil and gas for producing petrochemical products and products of commercial and industrial value.

Example of *reforming and blending operations* in a refinery can be the LPG being treated to produce propane and butane. Propane can be further chemically treated to produce propylene or butane can be chemically processed to produce isobutane, and ethane can be treated to produce ethylene. There can be numerous options and combinations for chemically treating various light cuts to generate products of industrial and commercial value.

The complexities of these products with their inherent properties and the equipment, plants, and chemicals required offer limited options to any business continuity planner for estimating and planning for continuity of operations, let alone the minimum level of continuity in operations.

There is also a direct cost implication for *heavy cuts* products to produce products of industrial and commercial value as these further require to be treated, as in cracking, reforming, and isomerization. The heavy cuts then get "transformed" into residue oil, asphalt, vacuum gas oil, fuel oil, vacuum residue, etc. These have their specific utility as industrial products, both as raw materials or as catalysts.

The *auxiliary operations* in the downstream processes are critical and need to be considered for their impact on organizational resilience, as these may have major noncompliance to environment aspects, production aspects, or utilities aspects. The BCM would also need to consider the other critical aspects. These individual factors that will have a bearing on the cost and implication of the BCM program in the refinery are listed here in a brief manner:

a **Environmental Aspect** – Covering air pollution, water pollution, noise pollution, the procedure for disposal of hazardous waste, and greenhouse gas emission effect.

b **Production Aspect** – Non-availability of crude/condensate, non-availability of sulfur recovery unit, non-availability of naphtha hydro treating unit, non-availability of distillation unit, or non-availability of desulphurization unit.

c **Utilities Aspect** – Non-availability of power, non-availability of cooling water, non-availability of natural gas and instrumentation air, non-availability of nitrogen gas and steam, or non-availability of desalinated water.

d **Other Critical Aspect** – Single vendor service risk, original equipment manufacturer dependency, single service provider, or interim risk due to technology upgrade in non-core processes.

From the above-listed aspects of auxiliary processes of downstream operations, it can be observed that each of the aspects has a debilitating impact on the production life cycle and other impact, including financial, environmental, and operational. All these aspects need to be considered in detail for developing a Plan B strategy, should there be an issue with the primary recovery strategy or Plan A for continuity.

It is important to note the requirement of equipment, spares, and ancillary requirement in the downstream production processes, whether in core or in auxiliary for continuing operations in case there is disruption in the primary processes or in case disruption is caused by a break in the supply chain for these in the production life cycle.

From the above contents, we are at a stage in downstream where the products of oil and natural gas are "ready to be taken to end-users/ customers" through various distribution channels.

For clarity in understanding the downstream operations, let us consider these operations further from the standpoint of the consumers, the customers, or the end-users of these products. Let us consider the aspect of retail and distribution as one stream and from the aspect of jet fuel airport operations. The retail and distribution operations cover the domestic demand, marine operations, as well as the commercial/industrial demand of the oil, gas, and petroleum products, and the airport operations primarily cover the fueling aspect.

For discussion purposes, let us consider the common aspects of BCM implementation challenges in both retail and distribution and in jet fuel airport operations. While these are being listed as common factors, there may be a difference in the level of complexity and gravity of risks and inequities with respect to the same factor. Let us delve into the details of these as follows:

1 **Multiple SPOFs in the Life Cycle** – In both segments, retail & distribution and airport operations, the nature of operations is so complex and depends on many unpredictable factors and vagaries, as elaborated earlier. These are factors that can jeopardize the entire operations in the respective life cycle of retail & distribution as well as in airport fueling operations. It is for these reasons that the business continuity planner must identify these SPOF during the stage of the respective business impact analysis (BIA), and the risk should get

addressed with a definite strategy of risk treatment, tolerance, transfer, or termination – the four Ts of risk management.

2 *Complex "Supply Chain" and "Supply Chain Risk Management"* – As the production of all products in oil and gas involves a long series of technical and chemical processes, its supply chain is fraught with risks, and also the business continuity planner will need to address the supply chain risk that can be triggered by a combination of factors, for example:

 a IT outage.
 b Lack of skilled staff or human illness.
 c Adverse weather.
 d Cyber risk and data breach.
 e Transport network disruption.
 f Insolvency in supply chain.
 g Outsourcer failure, etc.

3 *Very Heavy Cost of* **Plan B** *or Alternate Strategy* – The operation models in both retail & distribution and in airport fueling are unique. This is common in the processes and the plant and equipment utilized in the production life cycle. The planning for having an alternate strategy in case of any outage or disruption in the production process will require a heavy investment that may impact the financial viability of the project itself. Hence, it is essential that organization managements consider key aspects for the continuity of critical operations and may be required to perform a *balancing act* when considering *Plan B* or an alternate strategy for continuity.

4 *Complexity of End-to-End Operations Cycle* – The complexity involved in most of the oil, gas, and energy operations for extraction, production, transfer, loading/unloading, refining, distillation and fracturing, and conversion into final products and by-products is quite complex that the business continuity planner needs to consider a *Plan B* strategy for several processes and sub-processes. For the BCM planner, this can be an uphill task unless he/she is from the oil industry with the right experience to be able to accomplish this onerous task of developing alternate strategies for the multiple points and possibilities for outage and disruption.

5 *Culture as an Impediment* – Oil and gas is an industry with years and centuries of history, and its companies and personnel have been in the business for a long time. The history has "taught" many lessons to those in the oil and gas industry, and companies have adopted certain techniques and procedures for conducting business to be profitable and financially viable. These practices are further impacted by the

geographical locations and demographic combinations of the human populace engaged in the oil and gas industry.

6 *Legacy of "People, Systems, Vendors, and Suppliers, etc."* – As a natural fallout from the organization culture are the procedures and practices that are followed in the organization. After the organization has been in business for a considerable time, there are practices that become the norm for that activity or function, and these norms are difficult to change as at times these are the *unwritten rules promulgated by the management,* yet no one challenges them for fear of vindication. These kinds of issues pertain to the people in the organization, its systems and processes, its vendors and suppliers, etc. The business continuity planner during the stage of the BIA should analyze the impact of such practices on the operational performance and should endeavor to bring about a change when considering the continuity of its critical operations post a crisis, emergency, or outage.

7 *Diversity of Workforce* – The diversity of the workforce engaged in the oil and gas industry is so vast and varied that the individual nationalities, languages, behavior and habits, and cultural orientation are factors that need to be considered by the business continuity planner, so that the difference of these factors should not result in any event or incident that may cause disruption in the operations of the company. The mode and medium of communication need to be standardized so that there is common understanding of any "ground situation" and staff engage themselves in line with their designated roles and responsibilities following any emergency or crisis. These communication protocols must be agreed upon between the parties concerned and duly approved by the management.

8 *Criticality of "Response Time" Post Any Incident/Event/Outage* – In the event of any untoward incident or any outage happening due to any reason, the same needs to be anticipated for ensuring that the resulting *downtime,* instances of loss, loss of productivity, delay in delivery, or failure of customer commitment need to be considered for the recovery critical operations in the minimum earliest possible recovery time. Due to operational complexities in retail, distribution, and airport operations, the estimation of RTO is not easily determined, and in certain types of events and outages, the initial assessment and actions may take longer than normal time, and the actual damage and repercussions for the organization and its personnel may be substantial.

9 *Scarcity or Non-availability of Skilled Labor* – The oil and gas industries utilize a class of workforce that requires knowledge and training to address different risks and threats that are *part and parcel* with the operations in oil and gas. The inherent risks due to inflammable, toxic, and combustible properties of the products and

the raw material inputs to produce these products make it mandatory for staff and employees to adhere to procedures and the prescribed regulatory compliance. The workforce needs to be trained, and their skills and knowledge should keep pace with the time. There should be a schedule for training at regular intervals and refresher courses on a periodic basis.

10 **Understanding and Defining of RTO** – The events of the last few years have made it imperative that post any outage or disruption, the operations and availability of products and services must be made available, with the period of outage being reduced to the minimum. For this purpose, the organization that has imbibed BCM must identify *what is critical* while conducting the BIA and know about the critical operations, related dependencies, both internal and external, and the role and relevance of external providers, e.g., power, utilities, vendors and suppliers, etc. The BIA exercise should be undertaken with correct understanding of business continuity as a domain and the technical concepts of RTO, RPO (recovery point objective), MAO (maximum acceptable outage), MTPD (maximum period of disruption), etc. These and other terms should be familiar to the business owner and the business continuity planner so that the defined numbers that govern recovery of critical operations and operations resilience are determined in a systematic manner. The results of the BIA should be effectively used for planning continuity, and the outcome should be well-structured business continuity plans.

11 **Delivery Process Post Failure or After an Incident Has Occurred** – The processes post any incident that may impact the operations in retail, distribution or in airport operations have an important bearing. The processes that need to be adhered to are specific and approved that address *the downside to the business, if any*. Impact on the end customer and delivery of products and services should be anticipated by the business continuity planner, and plans and procedures must be in place to ensure timely delivery of the product and service within the pre-agreed timelines and approved RTO. It may be a worthwhile exercise for the business continuity planner to define the MBCO, which will in turn ensure that organization and its personnel are clear about the minimum service levels and minimum level of products to be delivered within the agreed timelines.

Following the discussion on the common factors in retail and distribution and airport fueling operations, let us now specifically delve into factors that impact the latter, namely retail and distribution, and the points that need to be considered from a BCM perspective are as follows:

1   *Heavy Cost of Maintenance* – The cost of maintenance of the plant and equipment to service retail customers is considerable due to the nature of the plant and equipment used and the critical point of safety and health risk to be adequately managed so that there is no incident that may compromise safety and regulatory compliance. Both retail and industrial demand of oil and gas products need to adhere to the minimum norms of safety features, quality, and specifications as per customer requirement or in line with the limits and parameters defined by regulators and health authorities. The safety aspect needs to be adequately made aware to the staff handling the product, including the risks and dangers of using a particular product, chemical, etc. There should be enough awareness and knowledge of the procedure to be followed in case of any incident of fire, spillage, vapor gathering, circumstances leading to breach flash point, etc.

2   *Cost of Spares and Alternatives Available* – As covered in #1 above, it is always a dilemma for the operations team to weigh between maintaining stock of critical spares and spare parts as an investment or call for the same by practicing *just in time* management. These decisions can greatly impact the business continuity strategy for the organization and can greatly influence how the teams perform during crisis and outage. A wait for a critical spare can make a lot of difference in terms of operations being resumed in a timely manner or operations being subjected to a *costly waiting period*. The business continuity planner needs to analyze all the pros and cons for the approach being followed for handling the requirement of critical spares. The planner should also see other possibilities along with business personnel to explore cheaper, more feasible, more practical, and time sensitive options of procuring spares and parts that can be used as substitutes without impacting the original asset and the quality of the product being produced.

3   *Correct Estimation of RTO* – The point is adequately covered in detail in the section covering retail and distribution, yet it is equally important for personnel to understand the relevance of RTO as a number, how it is determined, when should it be reviewed, what circumstances warrant reconsideration of RTO before its due time of review, and who should perform the review and the technical knowledge of the person deciding the RTO and the 360 degree impact of the RTO on the operations of the airport fueling and other airport operations. The business continuity planner must be able to understand, appreciate, and anticipate the effect of incorrect RTO being defined by the business and how this can have a catastrophic impact on the organization. This can impact its reputation, its market share, its customer confidence, its position of regulatory compliance, its legal and financial position, etc. Hence, the RTO for airport fueling operations should be carefully considered and

planned alongside customer requirements and the organization's financial viability.

4 **Concentration of Select Vendors for Critical Supplies** – Due to the age of the industry and the age of its *participants,* and considering the aspect of culture as covered in the preceding sections, there are certain practices that the business continuity planner must investigate and analyze. This is more so when the organization is dependent on its delivery based on sourcing of critical supplies from a single or limited sourcing points. There is a danger of over-reliance on a single source or danger of *taking things for granted while ignoring the writing on the wall.* There could be an instance of compromise of regular checks and controls due to the affinity factor. This single factor can be a source of SPOF in the operational chain in retail and distribution, and the business continuity planner should ensure that this does not happen and there is no collusion.

5 **Impact of Natural Disasters, e.g., Flood, Earthquake, Tsunami, etc.** – The impact of natural events cannot be understated from the point of business continuity. Yet, the business continuity planner must plan for basic and minimum operational recovery within the agreed time. The operations should also target to maintain the MBCO within the agreed timelines.

6 **Failure of Delivery Results in "Failure of the Customer Being Served"** – The business continuity planner of retail and distribution must anticipate and plan for instances of any delivery failure for any reason causing stoppage of work, disruption to operations, etc., and should work closely with the business manager to find acceptable solutions to ensure that customer requirements are met, if not immediately than within the agreed RTO. For instances where there is an extended outage due to crisis or situation at hand, the business continuity planner must assist the business owner in devising the action steps and pre-agreed option that will address the concerns of the customer and *buy time with the customer for delayed delivery or no delivery.* In any case, the business continuity planner should anticipate the likely damage the situation can cause, and the same should be covered by a mitigation plan cum strategy.

7 **Implied Risks due to the Inflammable Nature and Hazard Risk of Product Properties** – The inherent properties of the product make it imperative for the business continuity planner to consider the implied risk that may cause stoppage of work or disruption in operations that will have far-reaching consequences for all the stakeholders, namely the oil company, its customers, the civil and civic authorities, the insurance company, the community at large, etc. The business continuity planner must ensure that well-structured plans exist to

address this risk, and these plans should be kept up to date and reviewed for currency at regular intervals. The business continuity planner must also ensure that the contents of the plans are known to the concerned staff and that they are aware of their respective role/responsibility during an outage/crisis.

8 ***Implied Risks due to Human Error*** – Following the adage of *to error is human*, the business continuity planner must analyze the common types of errors in the production life cycle. This can be achieved by analyzing the "Help Desk" ticketing system or the referrals to IT and technology support personnel. The analysis can identify the root cause of the issue: Lack of knowledge, lack of training, etc. The business continuity planner should assist the operations teams in identifying these issues and jointly find a solution so that the risk of outage and disruption is reduced, if not eliminated.

9 ***Marine Operations:*** The importance of marine operations for the purpose of this book is being considered from both perspectives, namely the oil and gas industry aspect and from the perspective of the customer as the end-user of the oil and gas products. The cost involved in transport of oil and gas and other traded commodities is considerably cheaper than other modes of transport, namely by air or by land through road and railroads. As the "By Air" option is a costly option and the road and railroad options have limitations of connectivity issues and other aspects of e-commerce involving trade agreements and tariffs, etc., marine transport is the most popular one. For our purpose, we will consider the specific aspect of how BCM can be leveraged to ease the case of marine operations in the midstream operations in oil and gas. The important factors that a business continuity planner must bear in mind for assessing efficiency in the midstream are as follows:

a The type and nature of marine operations being conducted, for example, the type of ships being used, the intricacies of charter terms, conditions, and bindings of the charter agreement, insurance of cargo, insurance of crew/staff, etc.

b Cargo loading/mode of transport and unload at port(s) – terms and condition governing the loading/unloading, details of insurance of cargo and in-transit insurance, availability of transport, trucks at the destination port, and availability of ships and vessels for transfer/transport of marine cargo, etc.

c Export and import of oil and gas are regulated by laws and international regulations and governance as per country-specific norms, including provisions of the *Charter Party Legal Agreements*, which lay down the standard terms and conditions in the transport of the product using marine operations.

d   Impact of the pandemic on ship crew, which necessitates providing medical care for staff, their mental health, segregating the impacted staff, adhering to quarantine protocols, arranging for additional staff, etc. This also has a direct bearing on the cost of operations increasing substantially. The organization also needs to consider the extreme situation of "quarantine of the entire ship in the Anchorage due to pandemic positive cases on-board."

e   Docking issues for the ship with the cargo due to non-availability of berth or due to any other reason, including administrative and compliance issues.

f   Impact of weather extremities and unfavorable sea conditions affecting travel time and delivery schedules, leading to financial implications.

Having considered some of the common factors of concern from a business continuity standpoint in retail & distribution and in airport fueling operations as above and specific aspects relating to the former also as above, let us delve into the jet fuel airport operations for the points to be considered from BCM, namely:

1   *Complexity of Operation* – Starting from the receipt of crude up to the stage of delivery of jet fuel into the aircrafts, there is a long chain of oil life cycle. The journey goes from well-head to port, to refinery, to distribution plant, to pipeline/bridger/railroad, to delivery at an airport fuel farm with due quality check. The processes involved are complex concerning the specific quality, its color, its viscosity, its toxicity, etc.

2   *Understanding and Defining of RTO Is Extremely Critical* – Due to the nature of airport operations, it is extremely critical to arrive at realistic RTOs as any failure to do so will have a far-reaching impact on financial, operational, reputational, and legal consequences.

3   *Complexity in Defining the MBCO for Jet Fuel Operations* – This is more so due to the diversity and different types of crises and emergencies that can impact airport operations, and in each type of crisis the demands of the stakeholder may be different.

4   *Skill and Competence of Employees and the Resultant Inflexibility for Their Deployment* – Due to the nature of their work and their expertise, employees are skilled to perform a specific aspect of the operation that is unique in its requirement, and there are limited options for their re-deployment.

5   *Single Source Supplier for Critical Raw Material* – Due to certain key considerations and due to historical factors, the practice of using a single supplier is quite prevalent. These could be due to commercial considerations, *price lock-in*, legacy issues, *hassle-free dealings* in the

past, logistic considerations, quality of the product, etc. However, as the saying goes, it may not be prudent to "put all your eggs in the same basket."

6 **No Alternate Product to Substitute the Main Product** – Jet fuel is a unique product that has a very limited application and cannot be substituted for any other product. It therefore becomes imperative that all planning for a Plan B strategy in jet fueling operations needs to consider business continuity with the redressal of this issue to ensure continuity of fueling operations at the airport.

7 **Risk and Implications of "Contaminated Fuel" in the Airport Hydrant System (AHS)** – The risk of contaminated fuel in the AHS can have catastrophic consequences for all the stakeholders at the airport. These include the airport per se, the airlines operation from the airport, the fueling company, and the public.

In such a scenario, the airport operations in fueling of aircrafts needs to be stopped immediately, and the issue of contamination needs to be addressed on priority. The AHS has to be free of the contaminated fuel, and this may take considerable time. The airport authorities need to provide an alternate plan for continuing fueling operations. The alternative solution will need to be thought through in business continuity planning, and its practicality and feasibility need to be tested during non-crisis time. The consequences of contaminated fuel in AHS also have major cost implications, as well as legal and financial consequences, and penalty clauses may "kick-in" in case the BAU (business as usual) situation is not resumed after a reasonable period of time.

8 **Impact of Surge in Demand and Delivery of Fuel to the Aircraft** – Instances of surge in demand for fueling as a result of increase in commercial operations or due to any other reason can greatly affect the requirement and demand of jet fuel.

The underlying facts and reality have a cascading impact due to this surge in demand due to a war-like situation or any other commercial reason. This is also due to the limitation of physical infrastructure and complexities involved in transfer and transport of the increased demand. This is more relevant as the factors that need consideration are as follows:

a Capacity of the storage tanks at the source point.
b Capacity of the pipeline to transfer a maximum load.
c Capacity of the bridgers/tank trucks to transfer a maximum load.
d Legal and regulatory permissions required for the above, for transfer of hazardous & inflammable product via "public routes."
e Raw material shortage at the "processing source or start point."

9 *Issue of a Single Pipeline to the Airport* – Typically the location of airports in cities is quite different from the "processing source or start point," which is the refinery or a storage facility in the "tank farm," and these are connected through a single pipeline for supply of jet fuel. Any issue with the pipeline, be it technical or any other disruption due to human error, act of sabotage, or terrorist attack on the pipeline, can adversely impact the fueling operations at the airport. It is for this reason that an alternate Plan B for fueling operations must be planned. The complexity of the supply chain in oil and gas, along with the complexity in operations, add to a very high cost of Plan B for business continuity in the oil and gas sector. The culture and diversity in the workforce require a high level of coordination and collaboration. The oil and gas companies' unique issues and challenges add to the practicality of implementing business continuity in an effective manner. The numerous parties in the O&G sector operations add to the need for considering 360 degrees before going in for any specific strategy or solution to insure continuity of minimum critical fueling operations.

10 *Lack of Surplus Capacity or Assets at the Airport* – The infrastructure at the airport comprises:

a Storage Tanks.
b Airport Hydrant System.
c Fueling Trucks (for fueling from AHS).
d Tanker Trucks.
e Skilled Labor for Fueling Operations, etc.

The above can be a limiting factor to fulfill the fueling demand that may get impacted by increased requirements or due to shortage of assets.

11 *Requirement for Maintaining Strategic Reserve* – The requirement for maintaining a particular level of storage stock as a strategic reserve can be in line with a management decision, that may be agreed on by the management as a strategy for the future or for preparing for a future requirement not privy to the operations personnel. Another reason could be based on a directive from the government in line with its planning for meeting the requirement as envisaged by the government's future action. The reserve could also be built up for reasons of speculation and taking market position to benefit from a particular situation, e.g., economic consideration, commitment to the government, commitment to any counterparty, etc. While this could be a management diktat, it may not be easy for the business continuity planner to predict this build-up in reserve and its consequences.

However, the business continuity planner can indeed cover the point of the implication of the reserve build-up with respect to operational commitments and the delivery schedule to customers as these arrangements have a cost element attached and have to be taken into account in the normal production cycle. This would also impact the requirement of base raw material and the processing schedule over and above the levels of strategic reserves.

12 *Issue of Adhering to Government Diktat for Storage of Jet Fuel –* Instances of the requirement for maintaining stocks of jet fuel or increasing the storage quantity as per government directives is a factor that is difficult for the business continuity planner to estimate due to this requirement being temporary or ad hoc or driven by some other factors.

13 *Management Decision of Not Blocking Capital in Idle Stock of Jet Fuel and Its Operational Infrastructure –* Based on commercial, financial, or any other strategic reason, managements of organizations may decide in favor of maintaining higher stocks of jet fuel or to reduce the stocks to unblock the capital cost for the idle stock. There could be other reasons management may have for these actions, such as taking advantage of fluctuations in aviation fuel prices in international markets, change of supplier, maintenance of assets, etc.

14 *Implied Risks due to the Inflammable Nature and Hazard Risks of the Product –* due to the inherent characteristics of the aviation fuel being highly inflammable and combustible, it is important that the business continuity planner consider the aftermath of any incident involving fire. They must have a clear and approved strategy to deal with such situations.

15 *Criticality of Equipment and No Alternate Usage –* Fueling systems at airports are specialized equipment that adhere to the requirements of norms and regulations in this regard issued by aviation authorities. The equipment and assets used in fueling operations are sophisticated and monitor the quality of jet fuel, the presence of water and "air bubbles" in the fuel, and the presence of impurities in the jet fuel. All these are critical as their presence in the fuel can result in a major mishap for the aircraft.

16 *Fire Risk at the "Fuel Farm" at the Airport –* With the concentration of fuel stock in the storage tanks at the airport, there is a major risk of fire in the tank fuel farm caused due to a directly related issue or due to an indirectly related issue. A direct issue can be a fire in the storage tank fuel farm caused by accident involving mishandling of the product by tank farm staff. The indirect cause could relate to any other fire incident in the airport that may pose danger to the safety of the tank farm.

Examples of these can be a fire in the airport building, fire in the air traffic control tower, any aircraft, or any other transport mode on fire that is present at the airport. The business continuity planner needs to ensure that there are documented and approved plans to address these situations and the plans cover detailed procedures of what needs to be done and by whom, by when, and how it should be done. These crisis and emergency plans must be kept updated at all times, and the same should be reviewed on a timely basis. The business continuity planner in such organizations should be permanent personnel who should be aware of the nitty-gritties of airport operations and should be able to provide the right support to the business for ensuring critical operations are adequately covered for continuity and uninterrupted operations.

17 *Issue of Transferring Multiple Products in the Same Pipeline* – For organizations and countries, it may not be viable to have multiple pipelines for transfer of different products, and as the products are of similar class and domain, such operations yield more profits and are commercially more viable, for example, jet A1, petrol, diesel, gas, oil, etc.

18 *Implied Risks due to Human Error* – As the risk is like the risk in retail and distribution, please refer to #8 in the section covering retail and distribution.

19 *Complexity Involved in Arriving at "Insurable Value of Stock"* – As the demand for jet fuel is variable and dependent on many factors, as covered in the above-mentioned points, it is a challenge for the business continuity planner to arrive at the true value of insurable stock of jet fuel. The absence of the same can have direct financial and legal implications for the oil company and the airport authorities.

20 *Equipment Failure Leading to "Quality Risk" and Its Cascading Financial Implications* – From the preceding contents it is evident that the specific plant and equipment are required for performing effective fueling operations at the airport. In the absence of these equipment's functioning without any error or anomaly, the consequences can be fatal from a safety and health perspective.

The business continuity planner must ensure that the plant and equipment used in the life cycle of jet fuel are functioning accurately and there is near zero scope of error and, for the remainder risk, there are checks and controls in place to ensure the correct quality of jet fuel is supplied in aircrafts. The business continuity planner must ensure that maintenance schedule of the plant and equipment are adhered to, the parts and spares are replaced on a timely basis, and that no *short cuts* are adopted in this critical function at the airport. As these checks have major implications, namely legal, financial, social, commercial, and community related, the organization working with the business continuity planner must have two different sets of controls and checks to ensure that the end stakeholder interest is not compromised.

21 ***Cost of Emergency Response and Emergency Preparedness*** – Due to the risks involved and stakes involved in the safe working of an airport, it is extremely critical that the aspect of business continuity after any incident is carried out in a safe manner while involving all the relevant elements, namely the people, airport processes and procedures and effectively using the technology to continue the operations. This implies that some key aspects need to be addressed pro-actively. These would include creating the right awareness among airport staff and all other associated staff (of vendors, suppliers, service providers, staff representing civic and civil authorities, regulators, etc.) to be aware of process and procedures to be followed when facing a particular crisis situation – there to dos and don'ts.

As technology is the "biggest enabler," the business continuity planner must work with the technology team in devising specific and reliable IT disaster recovery (DR) plans addressing the needs of the airport staff in resolving the situation of crisis at hand. The IT DR plan solution should adequately cover the process capability on an as-is basis, on a "post crisis" basis, and whether the technology can support it in both scenarios.

Conclusion

This brings us to the end of this chapter, and from the elaborate narration, it is evident that oil and gas being the primary source of energy and the industry is of epic relevance when considered from a global perspective. The procedures and infrastructure involved in the production and distribution of oil and gas are extremely complicated, require a significant investment of capital, and require state-of-the-art technology. Owing to the complexity associated with oil and gas, it would take a more concerted intent and more toiling efforts to implement, establish, and govern BCM in O&G. This complexity also entails the contribution required from many professionals to come up with a meaningful and effective business continuity strategy addressing a plethora of causes that can jeopardize the operations and pose a threat to the very people and community it seeks to benefit.

While implementing business continuity and crisis management measures across the oil, gas, and energy supply chain, there are occasions that require hard decisions, primarily due to the cost factor and related benefits. The costs of any business continuity may be a huge investment to mitigate or reduce the impact of the risk, yet the benefit may or may not accrue as the same is dependent on a *downside contingent event.* This typically means that the organization may incur the heavy costs, as in take the insurance yet not realize the benefits of this insurance in the absence of any crisis, emergency, or outage happening. It is this dilemma that the management of the O&G company needs to address and find a fine balance between the pursuit of commercial and financial goals of the company viz-a-viz the interest and benefit of its human capital directly and the requirement of practicing safety for the community as prescribed by health and other civil authorities.

In true terms, there is no option for the O&G company management to not adopt and embrace BCM as the safety accompanying the products of oil, gas, and energy companies cannot be bartered. The critical aspects of inflammability, combustibility, and high flash points of the O&G components need to be considered for protection by way of adopting the option of *Plan B* for safely getting access to the products. Business continuity will help organizations and their management to come up with a *Plan B* solution that will provide a win-win position for all the stakeholders in O&G.

Developing Plan B in O&G is not an easy task and poses a challenge to all those involved in the O&G sector, though their impact and contribution may differ. In this pursuit, it is important to understand the role and impinging effect of the culture in its current state and also in the proposed solution. This is more so due to the fact that IT TAKES INDIVIDUALS TO MAKE AN ORGANIZATION, AND THEY ARE RESPONSIBLE FOR ITS SUCCESS. It is the people who "make it happen for any organization initiative to succeed or otherwise," and for this reason, it is said that business continuity has to be a *top down approach* with the right buy-in at all levels of the hierarchy in the organization.

As elaborated in the chapter, the finer aspects of the oil, gas, and energy life cycle and its supply chain components need to be understood and appreciated for a comprehensive business continuity strategy to address the multiple risks and threats that pose the danger of disrupting operations, impacting the O&G supply chain, causing a damaging effect in the quality of the product, causing an event snowballing into a crisis, and having a cascading impact on other sectors and the community. It is thus a very strong case that irrespective of the costs, efforts, finances, management intent, or commercial consideration – business continuity must be implemented in the oil and gas sector, and O&G companies must have formally trained personnel to manage this critical requirement, being guided by approved documentation that adheres to the requirement of the International Standard for Business Continuity (ISO 22301) or any national standard relevant in the country where the company has its operations. Finally, and as an afterthought, *let BCM be the beacon of light that stirs leaders to think beyond commercial returns and focus on contributing to society.*

Key Take-Aways

- The oil, gas, and energy life cycle, being very complex, requires very concerted effort from the organization to develop any business continuity strategy covering the life cycle.
- The oil and gas industry gets its contributions from many professionals comprising geoscientists, geochemists, geophysicists, engineering geologists, etc. Individual skill and experience need consideration in the organization's business continuity strategy.
- The multiple SPOFs need to be accounted for, and mitigation plans need to be developed.
- All streams in oil and gas operations, whether upstream, midstream, or downstream, are filled with risks and uncertainties that can jeopardize the core foundation of their respective organizations.
- The vagaries of oil price cannot be relied on for a definitive business continuity strategy for any organization.
- Core and auxiliary processes in the upstream operations are critical and offer a challenge to the business continuity planner.
- The dependency on vendors, suppliers, and service providers is crucial, and the business continuity planner should avoid over-dependence on one or a few of them.
- There should be enough and more than adequate awareness on safety protocols in the event of any mishap or any accident among the personnel across all levels of hierarchy.
- There is inflexibility in re-deployment of especially skilled resources; hence, backup planning must be very systematic.
- Single-source supply is a point of concentration of risk.
- Cost of emergency preparedness must be weighed against its prospective benefit.
- Due to the risks and threats to oil and gas being very dynamic, oil and gas organizations must be pro-active in assessing any emerging risk or any developing situation that may snowball into a crisis.

Chapter 8

Business Continuity in Hard Times

This chapter deals with business continuity management (BCM) as a management-focused initiative in any organization. The chapter delves into an important decision that needs to be taken by the Board and senior management in an organization relating to the implementation of the business continuity program in the company, irrespective of the fact that the company is in the green or in the red, yet it will implement minimum business continuity preparedness to ensure that the organization survives a crisis or emergency.

Corporations, like people, experience good, bad, and hard times. While referring to the good times for organizations, we mean that the company has enough money for a secure future and employee well-being. I am drawing a parallel for an organization's hard and bad times akin to an *empty stomach*, as in *an empty stomach or an empty pocket would teach a lot of lessons for survival*. I refer to it as the organization's hard times. If an organization is not having good things going, its focus and priorities will differ from those that are doing well and have a secure future. It can think of deserts and sweet dishes with its stomach full in the parlance of the organization's future when things are going well.

This chapter will discuss the opposite of *when the going is good for the organization*. This deliberation is necessary because most organizations plan and run orderly operations according to manuals and SOPs (standard operating procedures) that address compliance and regulations. Organizational staff in such companies *just need to do their bit* when business is good. Market position, market share, satisfied employees, customers, and stakeholders are all good. In these circumstances, the company should *go in for initiatives and projects that will increase the top-line revenues or reduce or maintain the bottom-line costs.*

As all organizations exist in a dynamic corporate environment that offers opportunities for growth and progress of the enterprise, it is equally manifested with risks and threats that hinder its growth and progress. The organization needs to consider the *downside of any incident* that can slow

DOI: 10.4324/9781003304678-8

down, retard, or stop it from growing. The growth may relate to an increase in operations, better financial returns, increased market share, an increase in team size, etc. The organization's risk manager and business continuity manager need to plan if the listed factors do not happen, and they should consider other strategies to remain in the business or call it quits.

It is prudent for risk and BCM managers to anticipate and prepare for facing disruption or outage caused by these risks/threats, and the organization must have strategies and continuity plans in place. Organizations in recent years, and more so because of COVID-19, are facing changed market dynamics and have altered the operating environment drastically. The resultant *New Normal* offers opportunities and challenges for organizations, who now need to prepare themselves for new situations considering the new risks, threats, and emerging market dynamics.

They will need to have alternate plans in case the first action step is ineffective and requires a changed strategy to deal with the crisis. One or more of the following factors may cause organizations to face difficult times:

1   Loss of the customer as a focus.
2   Disinterested or demotivated workforce and employees.
3   Inability to cope with market dynamics and social fabric.
4   Inadequate financial performance.
5   High rate of attrition and low employee morale over a period of time.
6   Fast action and decisions by competitors.
7   Inefficiencies in operational practices.
8   Disjointed organization culture.
9   Consistent low performance.
10   Mismatch of job role and personnel deployed due to attrition or for any other reason.
11   Weak supply chain risk management.
12   Failed management plans and strategies.
13   Lack of support and involvement of senior management.
14   Change in customer preference or requirements triggered by "new normal."
15   Obsolete and inadequate technology.
16   Internal dysfunctional factors.
17   Inability to face the aftermath of past incidents or outages and the vicious trade life cycle.
18   Increased payable.
19   Unrealized receipts/receivables.
20   Liability under contracts and legal agreements.

Although organizations would not choose the situations listed above, market conditions may force them to do so. If these situations arise, management will need a plan to resolve them or mitigate the damage. The organization must find a way to detect early signs of any of the above incidents or events.

When the organization is achieving its objectives and there is growth for the company, forward-looking initiatives and visionary projects can be undertaken to prepare the organization for its market position in the future. For these organizational initiatives to be successful, they need to be backed by:

1 Adequate budget.
2 Management intent and involvement.
3 Buy-in across the organization.
4 Transparency in management and governance.
5 Strong relationships in partnerships and alliances.
6 Cordial and congenial relations with regulators.
7 Common pursuit of the organization's mission and vision.
8 Practice of the organization's values in their true sense.
9 Adopted initiatives that have far-reaching effects on operations efficiency, customer relationship, market share, and market position.
10 Employees who feel motivated to *go the extra mile* and contribute to the interest of the organization.
11 Vendors and suppliers who are happy dealing with such clients with *no payment follow-ups and hassles*.
12 Companies that enjoy robust supply chain resiliency and operations that do not anticipate disruption.
13 Finances of the organization are free from the pressures of loans and interest default, have adequate working capital, and have funds available for capital projects and long-term funding.
14 Congenial relationship with regulators and government departments, as may be the case.
15 Investors and stakeholders have no issues in the management of such a company.

The above *happy and success factors* in organizations boost introspection for doing what benefits their staff, families, customers, investors, regulators, stakeholders, and *interested parties*. These initiatives are implemented when business as usual (BAU) is in effect and there are no deadlines. *Peace time initiatives* require careful thinking and planning to succeed while considering all angles. Such planning should be ideally done when there is no emergency, disruption, or crisis in the company and staff can dedicate time to *these higher organization pursuits in special initiatives*.

During peace time, management can focus on quality, energy savings, employee productivity, cost savings, revenue growth, customer satisfaction, and other initiatives. In a crisis or disruption, management must handle priorities and crisis response. If challenging and hard times and any issue listed above are impeding the operations and affecting the growth of the enterprise, management should accordingly deal with priorities.

What I am trying to draw the attention of readers, organizations, stakeholders, and management teams to is the *hidden opportunity* that exists in every difficult situation. We refer to these as hidden because the approach I am professing is for organizations to see the larger aspect; yet, only a handful of organizations are able to recognize these issues. In the words of Winston Churchill, *"one should never let a good crisis go to waste"* and it is easy for organizations to overlook what John D Rockefeller had stated, *"every disaster contains the seeds of an opportunity."* It is also said that "every crisis is an opportunity for the organization, provided it is ready to take steps to its advantage and be prepared in some way prior to the crisis." Such organizations should be prepared to handle any emergency and start their recovery from a point other than *from scratch*. Organizations may avoid direct losses if they are proactively prepared for crisis and disruption.

If such preparedness is lacking or incomplete, the consequences can be severe. An organization must have MINIMUM BUSINESS CONTINUITY PREPAREDNESS, regardless of its difficulties. Even if things aren't ideal, they must follow proper controls and procedures. Organizations that are flexible and adapt to current needs have a better chance of success and will be better positioned in the future. Therefore, we believe organizations should invest at least a little in BCM to avoid the *"last straw that broke the camel's back"* effect. By this, it is meant that adversity should not trigger events for the organization that will multiply its chances of liquidation and bankruptcy. If there is minimum preparedness using BCM concepts, there is a good chance that the organization has a minimum subsistence strategy and the right solution to address any risk or threat.

Business continuity embedment may vary for organizations that have it good and those that are struggling. The latter organization may need the minimum depth to survive a crisis or disruption and preparations to avoid catastrophic damage. Management of such organizations may utilize an analogy that *when a person is old and frail, it helps such a person to take vitamins, medicines, and health supplements*, which will maintain the person's basic health and give them the energy to conduct themselves. In relation to any organization also, we're talking about a much earlier stage – when a minimum BCM will help the organization respond to a crisis and protect its interests.

The minimum business continuity may differ from the preparedness as prescribed in ISO Standard (ISO 22301: The international standards for Business Continuity Management Systems) and refers to the organization having the basic business continuity norms in its framework. These may relate to an organization in difficult times having a broad business continuity policy, a simple business impact analysis (BIA), a comprehensive risk and threat analysis, and a clear business continuity plan (BCP). The BIA lists products, services, resources, technology, recovery time objectives, and internal and external dependencies. If the risk or threat materializes, risk assessment aids mitigation. If there is a disruption or outage, the BCP prioritizes business operations recovery and resumption. You will see that organizational personnel can meet the minimum business continuity requirement with little investment in a resource familiar with business continuity concepts and domain.

The approach that we are professing in this book is that organizations that are facing challenges, including ones that may currently be incurring losses, should implement a basic level of business continuity principles that will address the *weak links in the chain of the organization's survival.* There are additional advantages and benefits that the organization can realize in adopting minimum basic norms of BCM. Some of the advantages are mentioned here:

1 **Crisis Readiness** – Basic minimum business continuity readiness prepares the organization to be ready to face any crisis, though the degree of success may vary according to the intensity of the crisis and impact on the operations of the business.

2 **Identification of the Organization's Critical Business Operations** – Basic BCM will help the company identify activities, functions, and business operations that matter and should be cared for and resumed quickly in case of a disruption. Many criteria could classify this. These may include margin on sale, market position, legacy, history and emotions, market share, or any other relevant factor that makes the product/service relevant for the business owners and management of such organization.

3 **Risk Assessment for Critical Operations** – Once the key products and services are identified, as in (2) above, it becomes imperative for management to understand the downside of risks and threats that may impact the critical operations. Organization managements may decide to build mitigation plans to address these risks and threats so that the damage is less or is reduced considerably due to preparations being in place.

4 **Identify "Critical Dependencies"** – By doing basic BCM and BIA, which is simpler than that prescribed in ISO Standard, an organization can learn about its key products and activities, the resources needed for them, their recovery time objective (RTO) and recovery point objective (RPO), and most importantly, the dependencies

needed to prepare these end products/services. Dependencies can be internal or external and can be very damaging for the continuity of critical operations if the same are not considered properly and promptly. For appreciating critical dependencies, it is wise to have clear service-level details included. A pre-approved service-level agreement helps avoid confusion and provides *legal clarity* in the governance of external relationships between the organization and its vendor, supplier, service provider, etc.

5   *Identify "Critical Human Resources"* – In conducting the Business Impact Analysis, the organization can identify the key resources in the company and the critical ones that conduct the critical operations for the company. While adopting the basic BCM, the organization can also know the relevance of each role in operations and relate the same to its *Employee Retention Program,* working along with HR. Such identified key resources are at a higher risk of "jumping the bandwagon if they are not cared for or are unhappy about something in the Company" and need to be cared for, and for the critical ones, should be supported by clear growth and career progression plans.

6   *Identify "Areas of Improvement"* – By adopting basic BCM and performing the fundamental analysis to establish the minimum requirements for implementing and maintaining the basic business continuity model, organizations may be able to identify the points of "disconnect" causing issues of non-congruency in the operations process or production life cycle or in service delivery.

A closer look at the factors causing such issues may well lead the organization to understand the core issue, which may relate to staff requiring clarity of their roles and responsibilities, the need for training, issues with employee morale, non-redressal of HR issues, issues and practices hampering smooth operations, unaddressed operational issues having a negative impact on other/overall operations, inefficiencies of operational processes, etc.

The above factors can help the organization resolve issues when analyzing critical business continuity. The BCM analyst can also identify areas for improvement and improve solutions. Such solutions may have a wider impact on the organization, which can be used to improve staff efficiency and resolve issues effectively. A solution for an issue may also address the *rolling impact* of the matter on other issues.

7   *Improved "Future Planning and Strategy"* – Organizations do not exist in silos and are very much part of the corporate social fabric. They get affected by and influenced by the dynamics of the corporate environment and market conditions. While the organization adopts the approach of basic minimum business management implementation,

its management may be able to have a better understanding of the risks and threats to its line of business and its industry. In analyzing these factors in an objective manner and appreciating the impact of the analysis under BCM, for example, the business impact analysis, risk assessment to critical business, relevance of external dependencies, importance of strategic alliances, and need for important partnerships, the management may be able to review, revise, and improvise the organization plans and strategies for the future. Some of the key basic processes in business continuity can provide enough insight for senior management to understand the market situation – understand and analyze the risks and threats, including the emerging ones, to guide them through the scenario as it develops – and management can alter their vision, plans, and strategies accordingly.

8   *Positive Impact on Organization Culture* – While practicing the minimum basic requirements under business continuity, there exists an opportunity for personnel to imbibe the *values for surviving with the minimum*. By this I mean that organization personnel, while realizing the challenges facing the company and being an integral "part of the problem," also may realize that they *can be part of the solution*. This is more so as staff and employees are equally and adversely impacted when the organization is facing hard times, and its personnel must deal with different challenges each day. They also *need to survive along with the organization*. In this context, basic business continuity with good buy-in from across the organization changes the culture and behavior of staff and employees, who are themselves the impacted party and will benefit if the enterprise survives a crisis or emergency. Even a basic BCM implementation benefits employees and improves company culture.

9   *Improved Relationships* – Humans are more confident and optimistic when they know what the future holds. Due to basic business continuity and top management's positive outlook and disposition even during difficult times, organizational personnel's relationships improve because they know where the organization stands in the face of any untoward incident or crisis. Stakeholders – other staff, customers, vendors, suppliers, service providers, bankers, auditors, investors, regulators – are more certain of *what is going on in the enterprise and what they can expect based on transparency of the top management with respect to the organization's future*. There is positivity in the relationships among the stakeholders as they are based on trust, clarity of intent, and surety about the future.

10   *Improved "Supply Chain"* – The operations procurement team can identify supply chain management flow by implementing and maintaining basic business continuity and analyzing the production or

service life cycle. The supply chain must work smoothly to avoid disrupting dependent processes. Organizations must plan for interruption-related outages, which can be achieved by having two or more sources of supply, stockpiling, just in time procurement strategy, or any other method that will ensure continuity of critical operations. The major risks that can adversely impact the supply chain are as follows:

a   Lack of skilled staff.
b   Adverse weather.
c   Human illness.
d   Cyber-attack/data breach.
e   Transport network disruption.
f   Failure of outsource provider.
g   Insolvency in supply chain.

From the risk factors listed above, an exercise of basic business continuity can help the organization to have a *Plan B* for such outages, and the same should consider all possible aspects that can impact the outcome of the arrangement.

11 **Improved "Service Levels and Service-Level Agreements"** – BCM helps a company understand its operations with core detailing because of a properly conducted business impact analysis, where all timeline components are summed up as a single RTO number. A properly conducted BIA helps in correct evaluation of RTO with clarity of service levels between departments, external parties, and vendors/service providers.

12 **Better Positioning Post Covid** – The last three years with the pandemic – COVID-19 – most organizations, if not all, have faced volatility, complexity, and ambiguity in conducting their business and its uncertain future prospects. With widespread lockdowns plus global economic slowdowns, and falling economic growth rates, organizations worldwide faced unanticipated business situations. With a large work-from-home workforce, the organization's rapid digital transformation, high usage of technology, issues of confidentiality, issues of employee productivity, and the need for optimal investment in technology solutions and assets, the list is long. This has only made things complex for senior management, and it is burdened with decisions like *how to deal with so many issues requiring urgent attention and quick decisions.*

These risks and uncertainties, along with Covid-related issues, make it prudent for an organization to deploy a basic BCM system that will position the organization better to counter any crisis or emergency backed by a properly executed BIA and risk assessment for continuity of its critical operations. The basic BCM would include identifying minimum resources, timelines (RTO and RPO), dependencies (internal and external), and technology needed to complete the activity or function. Covid forced humans *out of their comfort zones* and forced organizations and their employees to explore new options that now drive the organization's future thinking.

13 **Countering Cyber Risks and Threats** – Three to five years ago, the world changed metaphorically, with technology advancement and innovation and Covid with its effects on humanity as two major factors. These factors have permanently changed how businesses operate. Changes have irreversibly altered the *old way of doing things*. In these circumstances, it is prudent for organization managements to take cognizance of the risk and threat scenario and weigh consequences of technology being unavailable, thereby crippling enterprise operations. Organizations should be prepared with strategies to protect their interests.

Technology and its application have opened many doors for opportunists to multiply the effectiveness of technology and also for negative players and threat vectors to carry out their malevolent intentions and cause damage and losses. Covid-induced technology investments necessitated office decongestion, staff working from home, and operations spread across multiple offices with increased operational locations. Increased remote workers have increased the operational span for HR, finance, operations, sales, administration, and procurement departments and have also increased the organization's cyber risks. Cyber risk, or cybersecurity risk, is any potential exposure for loss or harm due to an organization's information or communication system being breached. With the rise of threat actors and the sophistication of their attacks, management must address this risk.

Any organization's minimum business continuity solution should address the urgent need for sophisticated malicious cyber-attack controls. Senior management must recognize the increased variety of threat actors and their innovative ways of attacking, and IT managers must anticipate and counter threat actors ranging from downloaders to coders to organized crime and hackers to cyber mercenaries. The organization's IT infrastructure and network should be protected. Even with minimal business continuity implementation, IT should be able to anticipate the possible impacts of these threats and risks and know the attack's potential outcomes, such as creating nuisance for users, data breach/theft, denial of services, financial fraud, identity theft, etc. Organizations should analyze these threats during "peace time" to prepare for cyberattacks.

14 ***Cloud Solution as an "Option for Cost Saving and Optimization"*** – The events of the last decade have changed how organizations do business, and their dynamic environment offers new opportunities and is also plagued with risks and uncertainties. Technology choices and strategies have changed with innovation, and technology deployment in *"unexplored waters"* have made this possible. An organization's TCO (Total Cost of Operation) primarily depends on technology, so it makes sense to constantly seek *cheaper, re-engineered, practical, faster, and more optimal and viable technology options*. Organizations need to find and adopt alternative options in the long run.

BCM, even in its basic form, can help a company learn the "nuts and bolts" of its technology. Its IT manager knows the revenue and capital IT-related costs, and Cloud technology may help the company overcome its IT system costing issues. The Cloud option may enable the continuity of crucial IT services online. This option allows flexible IT solutioning to support business lines based on clear service arrangements between the organization and cloud service provider. Lower IT and technology costs may benefit the organization and help simplify top management decision making despite many challenges and a poor financial situation. The BC manager and IT Manager can work together to find a better cost solution and invest in the company's future.

15 ***Capitalize on the Findings of Basic Business Continuity Implementation*** – There has been a lot of debate on the actual benefits of implementing BCM, be it direct or indirect. Its importance cannot be undermined as a one-time gain for a one-time initiative only. Business continuity implementation in its basic form helps organization management to:

a   Resource requirements for critical operations.
b   Optimal utilization of the organization's limited resources.
c   Identify weak links in the joint working of the organization's people, process, and technology.
d   Identify critical dependencies in its operational processes.
e   Validate its RTO and RPO to understand the organization's crisis readiness.
f   Confirm if the SLAs (Service-Level Agreements) are in sync with the aspect of continuity of the critical operations.
g   Minimum business continuity implementation helps its finance department to have a better *hold on the spend and expenses*.
h   The organization has knowledge of the current vulnerabilities in technology with a properly conducted IT risk assessment.
i   With minimum BCM, the organization has the maturity and understanding of the linkage between IMP (Incident Management

Plan), ERP (Emergency Response Plan), CMP (Crisis Management Plan), BCP, IT-DRP (IT Disaster Recovery Plan), and MRP (Media Response Plan). The knowledge of linkage can determine a prompt or delayed response of the organization during crisis or emergency, *when every minute counts and can impact saving of life with timely action.*

j   Identify *"concentration risk"* of dependency on a single supplier source, single vendor, or single service provider, which can be a *showstopper during crisis or emergency.*

k   Identify what is critical, including identification of key staff, key assets, and critical suppliers and providers.

l   Key human resources, building, and infrastructure required for continuity of critical operations, etc.

m   Manage operational supply risk management in an effective manner to have a smooth feed to production life cycle.

As shown above, business continuity can help senior management, teams, and departments overcome their challenges. BCM considers risks and threats to its critical operations from a 360-degree perspective and expects the business continuity team/manager to develop mitigation strategies for these threats and risks. Thus, in difficult times, a minimum level of BCM is safe.

16   **Developing "Early Warning Signals" Prior to Any Crisis or Disruption** – While adopting the minimum business continuity option, the same can help in preparing the organization to be ready for facing any crisis or emergency. While covering the previous point to *capitalize* on the findings of basic business continuity implementation, we covered how BCM can help an organization in dealing with a crisis or emergency and the various inputs to organization management when practicing business continuity. It is also relevant in this context that BCM teams and managers, while developing strategy for crisis handling, may also have a built-in mechanism of incident identification for the type of incident and its impact on the operations of the company. These *early warning systems* can be of immense value while the organization deals with its challenges and yet come out successful in overcoming a crisis or an emergency.

17   **"Putting Your Dollar Where It Matters Most"** – This phrase is being used to stress the importance of spending every dollar in a cautious manner so that the organization realizes value in every dollar it spends towards its intended benefit and towards dealing with the difficult times the organization is facing. It also implies that once the organization has adopted the basic minimum business continuity,

the management and its personnel know what resources the organization possesses and how these limited resources need to be utilized in an optimal manner to yield the maximum benefits in the interest of the enterprise.

18 **Improved Communication** – Minimum business continuity allows an organization's staff to prepare for any crisis with a plan that outlines their role and responsibility for critical operations continuity and resumption. The BCP also includes details on how to analyze any incident and trigger action steps based on its type, impact, and nature of the incident.

The plan's actions occur with proper information exchange about the event/incident. Such communication is tested during peace time and can be invaluable in crisis. Communication helps the organization whether it is having a *good time or having challenges* when it practices business continuity. These communication protocols should not be *paper plans alone* but should be practiced so that staff in the *communication chain* know who to contact in emergencies and what to say. Effective communication during crisis exercises can help the team handle crises.

19 **Better Management of Product and Service Life Cycle** – As the organization embraces BCM, it will stand to gain from the benefits of it, and its managers can better understand the factors that may be impeding the growth, development, and realization of the full potential for the organization. BCM helps in *breaking down* the complex factors into simpler factors that can be addressed in a systematic manner. This is possible as a result of a properly conducted business impact analysis and proper risk assessment of threats to its critical products, services, and operations.

20 **Faster and Considered Management Decisions** – Management priorities differ for organizations that are *doing well* and those that are *struggling*. Management of an organization that is struggling through difficult circumstances and obstacles is concerned that *they are not missing anything that may cost the organization dearly in case something critical gets missed.* To conserve resources and maximize efficiency, management is cautious. With basic minimum business continuity, it can anticipate the negative effects of any event or incident and better understand the risk scenario and build safeguards to protect its critical operations. Because of structured plans and documents that outline what to do and what not to do in a crisis, senior management can make faster and better decisions to protect the organization.

Conclusion

From the elaborate narration of the possibilities made possible by adopting and implementing the minimum basic characteristics of BCM, organizations can build a *wall of confidence* wherein the minimum tenets of business continuity will establish the plans, procedures, protocols, and awareness in organization personnel to act responsibly during any outage or crisis. Business continuity norms prevent crises and emergencies from *causing a multiplier effect, leading to the liquidation of the organization already facing challenges and hard times, primarily financially.* With management already struggling, any outage or disruption may have a *double-whammy* effect and throw the enterprise into disarray if BCM is missing. In a chaotic environment where management must make *hard decisions,* one wrong decision can have a cascading effect, with the following events also having a negative impact. Basic BCM can provide resilience options for the organization.

Key Take-Aways

- Crisis requires a quick management decision.
- It helps organizations to consider the *worst-case scenario* in BAU and plan accordingly.
- Minimum business continuity will prepare the organization to have plans and strategies to deal with any crisis and emergency.
- Organizations facing challenges and adopting minimum business continuity have better control of their limited options for conducting their operations.
- Organizations should have *Plan B* in view of increased risks and threats.
- For optimized technology costs, cloud may offer the solution; however, minimum BCM lets the organization weigh the pros and cons of cloud computing and its feasibility.
- Minimum BCM enables the organization to formulate *early warning systems* that trigger actions prior to an incident resulting in or snowballing into a crisis.
- The minimum BCM helps in *better utilization of every investment* being made, and managements are in control during crisis/emergency.

Chapter 9

What Should HR Consider in Hiring Business Continuity Manager?

For a business continuity program's successful implementation and for it to serve the intended purpose for the organization, a lot depends on the personnel in the organization implementing it in terms of their commitment to the program, possessing the right skills and experience to understand the requirements and technical nuances of business continuity and crisis management domain. Knowledge about the subject aids the personnel in performing their job responsibilities effectively. This chapter describes the points that organization HR must know and follow for hiring the right business continuity management (BCM) resource.

It is seldom that we find that organizations having implemented BCM have inadequate readiness and the ability to effectively handle any crisis or a disruption. This is so, although BCM is considerably *old in age* from the time it was initiated in the organization. There could be many reasons for this situation wherein there is incongruency in the working of the organization's people, process, and technology while dealing with any crisis or emergency. Traditionally, the organization's core business processes have been dependent and driven by technology, but in the last two decades, this technical focus has changed to compliance and strategy focus for the continuity of the organization's businesses.

In this chapter, we will be focusing on *What should HR consider in hiring a business continuity manager?* It is important for organization management to realize that, just like any other management system, it needs to be properly understood and then implemented following the basic tenets for achieving the objective of enhancing organization resilience.

BCM as a focus area for organization management has gained traction in the last two decades with some major disruptions across the world, with the major ones being the 9/11 World Trade Center attack in New York in 2001; hurricanes Andrew and Katrina in USA; terrorist attacks in various countries (USA (9/11), London (7/7), Istanbul, Bolan,

DOI: 10.4324/9781003304678-9

Madrid, and Mumbai (26/11), to name a few; natural calamities of floods, earthquakes, and snow storms; COVID-19; the Russia–Ukraine war of 2022; and countless incidents that have impacted society at large across the globe.

Puzzle of Hiring the Right BCM Professional

It is in this context that I wish to draw the attention of HR directors, their managers, and their teams to the specific skills, experience, and qualifications required to hire the right candidate as BCM manager of the company. For this purpose, I refer to some questions and answers that hold the key to the right hiring. The honest answers will address the issue of the person with the right ability and overall disposition with the correct attitude and experience to be employed with the clear objective of leading and enhancing organizational resiliency.

The questions in this regard are as follows:

1   Does the prospect understand:

   - What is BCM in its true sense?
   - How is BCM related to other management information systems (MIS)?
   - How does management interpret and utilize the output of various MIS?
   - What BCM inputs are required by management during a crisis, emergency, or disruption?
   - What is the correlation between incident management, emergency response, crisis management, business continuity management, IT disaster recovery, and media management?

An important aspect to understand is that it is equally important for HR personnel to be aware of the pointers listed above. It is often observed that due to lack of total clarity on the above-listed points, HR is unable to assess the requirement from both sides of demand (of the business units) and the supply side (possible BCM hire). A good way to overcome this hurdle is for HR to draw a clear job description (JD) that will address *What does the business expect from a BCM professional?* and *What is the prospective BCM professional expected to deliver?* A cut-copy-paste from the Internet is indeed an option that the HR personnel should avoid, as this may not cover all the specific aspects of the BCM job requirement.

2   Does the prospect have the **capability to understand the core business** of the Company and whether he/she has the capacity to understand the priorities of business operations?

3 Does the prospect know **what it would take to run the critical operations** of the Company and how to manage affairs during interruptions in a way not to escalate into a crisis?

4 Does the prospect have experience and understanding of **Comprehensive Coordination** of companies' operations during crisis and emergency?

5 Ensuring the prospect possesses some **key personality traits** to be successful as a BCM personnel:

    a Adequate domain-related academic qualification.
    b Ability to utilize his/her experience for optimal BCM solution.
    c Eye for detail.
    d Logical – ability to see the larger picture.
    e Analytical, thinker, and innovative.
    f Fast learner and good listener.
    g Influencer.
    h Motivator and sensitive.
    i Amenable and approachable.

6 Does the prospect demonstrate the ability to recognize and **differentiate between social and technical characteristics** of a business interruption?

7 Does the prospect know **what contribution is required from a BCM manager** during a crisis/emergency?

8 Does the prospect have an **understanding and ability to analyze salient phases** as a crisis emerges and the various points for intervention to limit the impact of the threat?

9 Does the prospect understand the **needs and requirements of different stakeholders**, along with their specific needs during a crisis and emergency?

10 Does the prospect have it in him/her to **bring together the internal/external stakeholders** while managing the crisis/emergency effectively?

Puzzle of Right Assessment of BCM Professional

The HR team in any organization should be able to *extract* and get the right information from their prospective hires to validate their specific skills and experience and its *mapping to the job at hand*. It is of critical importance for the HR team to be convinced that *what is mentioned in the CV and resume of the prospect gets reconfirmed during HR-Prospect interaction,* and HR should *ask the right questions to get the right answers from the prospects*. BCM being a specialized domain, it is useful to get answers to basic queries such as *What was your role in the solution*? How *did you do it? What challenges did you face? What was your basis for achieving project objectives? etc.*

It is seldom that the organization's proper due diligence at the time of hiring and recruiting business continuity aids in proper continuity of business and correct handling during a crisis. It is also very relevant for this validation by HR personnel to know and understand the key steps of business operations. This awareness will immensely help in their analysis in corroboration of facts with the actual experience of the prospect.

The HR team should be able to validate that the prospect is a candidate who can effectively manage the context of the BCM program across the organization with knowledge and clarity regarding what it takes to initiate BCM, understanding of the steps involved in planning for business continuity, its governance and implementation, and its operational management. Coupled with these abilities, he/she should be able to understand and implement legal and regulatory compliance.

The complexities increase drastically when HR needs to recruit a person in a senior leadership role to assist the senior management personnel during a crisis. The personnel are expected to *advise and support* the senior management, including timely inputs during crisis for their right and timely decision. It is for this reason that HR's role assumes a key importance in the hiring as any bad decision or judgment will affect the organization during any future crisis/emergency, by which it may be too late to protect the company from damage to its reputation, market share, or stakeholders' interest, etc.

Puzzle of Relating Incident-Emergency-Crisis and Business Continuity Situations

Today the dynamics of the business environment are changing so fast that what is relevant today for the organization's focus may change over a short period of time due to changed market scenario, innovation, and development in technology or due to changed priorities and altered vision of the organization. It is due to this reason that organizations need to monitor the risk and threats that could interrupt their business and impact their operations, alter their financial position/potential and cause customer attrition. Accordingly, the concept of organization resilience is broadening to include risk management, crisis management, business continuity management, and IT Disaster Recovery. The role of a crisis manager or a business continuity manager or by any other name the organization chooses today covers all these functional responsibilities, and HR must take these specific requirements in to consideration when hiring BCM professionals.

HR in organizations should have an understanding of how technology has impacted the function of business continuity, which has changed from pure IT focus to value-chain focus, from being an IT staff responsibility to a multi-disciplinary team responsibility, from protecting core operations to protecting the entire organization, from sustaining the current position to the stage of creating sustainable advantage, from the traditional parochial view to open system view, and lastly, from an emphasis on recovery to emphasis on prevention. It is in this context that HR should understand the role of the BCM professional in incident management, emergency response, crisis management, and business continuity enabled by using appropriate technology solutions.

Puzzle of Benchmarking

From the preceding discussions, it may be prudent for HR to understand the job requirements with a good understanding of the company's business operations. It is in this context that the organization's HR should follow established norms as a clear basis for assessing the competency of the prospective BCM personnel. A good benchmark for easy understanding and reference is the UK's Business Continuity Institute's "Competency Framework", that defines the professional standards required for effective performance as a BCM practitioner. Using the framework HR can help in developing resilience capability through resource planning, deployment, and development. The framework contains 12 competencies relevant to BCM, that are segregated as *Leadership & Management (L&M) competencies and Professional Practice (PP) competencies*. Ethics and values are a common competency in the framework. The L&M competencies relate to working with others for a productive outcome, inspiring leadership, thinking innovatively, and creating an internal and external environment for successful BCM program implementation. The PP competencies relate to the skills needed for the six professional practices in the BCM life cycle. The practices of Policy and Program Management, Embedding, Analysis, Design, Implementation, and Validation can be studied in detail by browsing www.thebci.org.

HR personnel should be wary that both competencies are documented and clearly understood for the right hiring of a BCM professional. They should know the relevance of traits of the BCM professional to be an impactful communicator, an influencer, a motivator, a problem-solver, collaborative, sensitive, a relationship builder, and to anticipate *tomorrow* with due analysis of risks and threats. He/she should be able to understand, interpret, implement, and maintain the BCM framework as per the BCM life cycle of defining the BC Policy & Program, embedding BC awareness across the entity, analyze and design an optimal BCM solution that gets tested and validated in subsequent stages in the BCM life cycle. HR personnel should endeavor to hire as per pre-approved process and *not try to invent wheel with every new hiring*.

Conclusion

From the preceding content, it can be logically inferred that the organization's HR needs to have the right understanding of the business continuity domain and the right criterion in assessing the candidature for any prospective hiring of business continuity personnel. Although HR personnel are not expected to have a deep understanding of BCM, they should understand the basic requirements that need to be complied with in each stage of the BCM life cycle. They should be able to discern from the job description and its relation to a candidate's CV detailing the candidate's skill and experience and whether it matches the requirement of the organization, wherein the business continuity personnel are adding to the organization's resilience during crisis or emergency.

As a proactive measure, HR personnel should do a market benchmarking to ensure that the *enterprise resource is equipped with the latest update of technology and any other practice that will help them deliver their best.* The HR team should partner with the BCM team to proliferate BCM awareness sessions regularly and organize BCM and refresher training to personnel involved in running and maintaining the critical operations of the enterprise.

Key Take-Aways

- HR team/personnel must have appropriate understanding of BCM and its life cycle.
- HR, while selecting the BCM professional, must correlate the candidate's skill and experience to the resiliency requirement of the enterprise.
- HR should be able to perform training need analysis (TNA) for assessing the BCM awareness of employees across the organization.
- HR personnel should be adept in benchmarking the organization requirement to established standard competencies.
- The character traits of staff having a role in the organization BCM framework should be tested regularly to ensure that enterprise interest is not compromised during a crisis or emergency.

Chapter 10

Supply Chain Risk Management
The Silent Lifeline for Success

COVID-19 has impacted organizations across sectors, industries, and countries. The very operating model has been altered for organizations to sustain the *pressure of their New Normal*. Events of the recent past COVID-19 and the Ever-Green Suez Canal blockade in March 2021 have highlighted the significance of supply chain resilience like never before. Business continuity (BC) and risk management (RM) need *re-thinking* in their approach and focus for organizations to have a resilient supply chain in their BC strategy. Boards and top managements in organizations across the globe (based on the global impact of COVID-19 and the recent near-scare due to the Suez Canal blockade in March 2021) need to *reassess and re-think* how the business will be conducted in the near and long term.

The leadership and senior managements of organizations need to comprehend the *macro scenario* of the correlation between supply chain management (SCM), RM, BC, and crisis management (CM) and how each of these can contribute to the organization being *crisis ready*. There is an urgent need for organizations to come out of the situation of doing a balancing act while considering and adapting to multiple factors to *remain relevant and competitive*.

It is becoming more widely acknowledged that the sustainability of supply chains is an essential driver of company value as well as an essential component of effective corporate responsibility performance.

Firms have begun to build programs to address supply chain sustainability since the 1990s, when big consumer brands in the West faced scandals and campaigns highlighting bad working conditions in their supply chains. These scandals and campaigns focused on the companies' supply chains. As the area has expanded, prominent organizations have increasingly understood that these initiatives do more than deflect unwanted stakeholder attention; supply chain sustainability may provide commercial value. This realization has come about because of the growth of the sector.

Today's corporate denizens have witnessed incidents and events that are of diverse genre and have resulted in disruptions that primarily impacted

DOI: 10.4324/9781003304678-10

their SCM. SCM is an integral part of any organization's production or service life cycle. Supply chain sustainability helps management in managing the social and economic impacts of good governing practices throughout the life cycle of the company's goods and services, which in turn results in enhancing the value for all stakeholders.

In this chapter, we will analyze the critical aspect of supply chain risk management (SCRM) for an organization and how its mismanagement can lead to a situation akin to enhanced risk or a basis for crisis or a cause for disruption of business requiring invoking of a BC Plan. For ease of understanding of the reader, the author has bifurcated the different aspects of SCRM, namely:

a   Understanding the common elements.
b   The leverage between BC, RM, SCM, and CM, followed by.
c   Analysis of the aspects of congruence from SCM perspective.
d   The new and real issues along with common imperatives across the domains, and.
e   Different SCRM strategies for effective response and recovery.

Common Elements

All the domains under consideration, namely BCM, RM, SCRM, and CM, are characterized by elements that affect these domains, though their degree of impact and relevance may differ among each other. These common elements are as follows:

1   Risks, Threats, and Uncertainty.
2   Disruption and Outage.
3   Need for Protection.
4   Need for Optimization.
5   Impact on Market Share.
6   Impact of Emergency or Crisis.
7   Protection of Reputation.
8   Alternate Continuity Plans.
9   Relevance of Teamwork.
10   Requirement for Regulatory Compliance.
11   Need for Adequate Awareness for Right Confidence.
12   Relevance of *People, Process and Assets*.
13   Importance of *Robust SCM*.

From the points listed above, it can be inferred that BCM-RM-SCRM-CM are entrenched together as they can be any of these factors individually or collectively. It is important to note that during any crisis or emergency, all 13 factors listed above, will need to be analyzed per their individual consideration, e.g., Uncertainty and its corresponding alternate plans will be needed for BC, RM, SCRM, and CM for a particular incident type. For example, impact and dealing with a situation like fire or power outage, etc.

The Leverages and Its "Chain Impact"

From the factors listed above, it is only prudent on the part of organization management to consider the conundrum of BCM-RM-SCRM-CM with a common *paint brush* for a comprehensive solution, coordinated efforts with a planned approach with collaboration among the different teams in the organization. By doing so, there would be little or reduced risk of a surprise during any crisis. Such a unison of efforts is also essential for collective gains from the applicable 13 above-listed factors.

When a management team does this comprehensively, it can achieve larger benefits for the organization as an entity, namely the following advantages:

1 Well-established alternate plans.
2 Proper compliance to regulations.
3 Better stakeholder management.
4 Optimization of resources (both life and non-life).
5 Protection of human life, company assets, the company's market share, and the company's reputation.
6 Well-considered SLAs with vendors, suppliers, and service providers.
7 A common communication setup and protocol across BCM-RM-SCRM-CM domains.
8 Importance of organization reputation in any situation of BCM-RM-SCRM-CM.
9 Significance of a robust supply chain during SCM and CM.
10 Relevance of economies of scale in operations, especially when dealing with a crisis.

The leverages among BCM-RM-SCRM-CM are of equal importance, especially when one analyzes from the supply chain perspective. The supply chain aspect should be accounted by management, as there are several factors that have a *multiplier effect* when the organization is dealing with a crisis, a BC situation, or with risk or a SCRM issue. If any one of the following impacts one of the domains of BCM, RM, SCRM, or CM, it may have a crippling effect of stoppage of operations in the other domain. For example, an IT outage may result in stoppage of critical operations and have a consequent impact on its financials, operational capability, breach of regulation, etc. A well-considered list of these factors is captured hereunder:

a   Availability of skilled workforce and the impact of "missing experienced personnel on the floor" can disrupt operations immensely.
b   Impact of employees falling ill or when they are sick.
c   Impact of weather extremities.
d   Impact of technology outage or network connectivity.
e   Incidences of cyber-attack and data breach.
f   Disruption in transport network and related logistics.
g   Insolvency of any party in the organization supply chain.
h   Requirement of adhering to new laws, rules, and regulations.
i   Incidences of natural shortages and scarcity of material required as input.
j   Any failure in the outsourced function or activity.

The Leverages Demystified

It can be observed from the leverages and the chain impact that while thorough planning can bring out the best in an organization's ability to deal with crisis, emergency, disruption, and outage, it can also have a very damaging impact on the enterprise if the same leverages are not dealt with appropriately by the management. The same factor of blessing can become a hindrance to its success. These factors can cause *derailment from the purpose of the organization*. As one considers the thin line of SCRM and its *deathly blow on the operation's belly* can have a radical and harmful impact on the very existence of the organization. Some of the important factors are listed hereunder:

1   Disruption in the procurement process.
2   Requirement for trained and experienced manpower.
3   Need for coordinated communication as per pre-defined protocol.
4   Need for *Plan B* for sourcing and SCM.
5   Requirement of proper vendor management.
6   Impact on supply due to the global economic situation.
7   Need for preparing organization IT infrastructure for combating cyber risk threat.
8   Need to take advantage of leveraging strategic alliances and partnership during the crisis/emergency.

The Common Imperatives

In dealing with crisis, BC issues, risks or threats, or a SCRM issue, there are common imperatives that can be dealt with jointly, thus saving costs, management time, and resources for a coordinated and comprehensive solution. With a structured approach, organization management can manage and be in control during these testing circumstances.

The factors that need to be considered are as follows:

Documentation

All the required documentation in the four domains should be there duly approved by the management. The documentation should address the five Ws and one H (What, Where, Why, When, by Whom, and How).

Currency of Plans

It helps the organization immensely when it has updated and co-ordinated plans for dealing with crisis, BC situation, or a risk/threat. The plans, while being updated, should be fulfilling their purpose by supporting the other management plans for their success during crisis and emergency.

Early Warning System

A well-established and successfully tested solution for early warning helps the organization in taking and initiating timely action, invoking safety measures to reduce and limit the loss due to disruption and outage. The early warning may also help the organization in protecting its reputation, its stakeholder interest, and its *market share*.

Training and Awareness

The knowledge of current processes, procedures, and awareness of their respective role and responsibility helps the organization and its employees in effectively dealing with the crisis or emergency without confusion and with clarity of purpose.

Top Management Commitment

It always helps in the situation of crisis and emergency to have the com-mitment and buy-in of the senior managers and top management. This ensures that management is aware of the possible outcomes during any crisis, and organization is better placed in terms of any urgent requirement for a quick decision during the crisis. With the anticipation of the down-side of any outage, the team can react faster and expedite action to protect the interest of the company.

Lessons from Real Life – Its Rolling Impact on SCM

While devising a plan for BCM-RM-SCRM-CM to deal with crisis irrespective of the domain nomenclature, the organization must not lose sight of the environment that is beset with risks and threats. The reality of these risks needs to be accounted for in the preparation and pre-planning for crisis. The years 2019 onwards until now have exposed human society to the risks of the pandemic (due to COVID-19), the extreme situation of disrupted global supply chain (e.g., due to the Suez Canal blockade for over a week in March 2021), risks posed by cyber threat and the ongoing Ukraine-Russia conflict (since February 2022), etc.

These uncertainties have posed challenges; some of the notable ones are mentioned hereunder:

a   Increased cost of operation.
b   Increased procurement cost.
c   Need for additional *sourcing points*.
d   Increased cost of insurance.
e   Need to relook into finance and cost.
f   Need for management to make a *quick decision*.
g   Need for enhanced compliance.
h   Rethinking on investment in technology.
i   Counter measures for cyber risks, hacking, phishing, etc.
j   Accounting for thw impact of *political climate and economic environment*.
k   Pressure to reduce costs with the option of cloud solution and its related risks of governance, legal remedy in case of breach of contract by different providers, and the resultant *workforce of skilled unemployed*.

The Alternative – How Can SCRM Aid in Better BC PC Plans, CM, and Effective Response and Recovery

The SCRM has evolved to offer some tested and proven alternatives that have helped in strengthening the enterprise supply chain while also devising more practical and achievable BC and CM plans. The strategies also give the mitigation plan options, which use technology as an enabler, enhancing the organization resilience. These options are as follows:

* **Mapping of the Supply Chain Heat Map** as an RM technique refers to the company's supply chain design represented as a model with risk points duly identified and represented as a heat map across the organization's SC. The heat map is color coded to depict the level of risk, with red associated with high risk, yellow/orange for medium risk, and green for low risk. A simpler *Mapping of Supply Chain* is a graphical representation

of firm's tier-one and sub-tier suppliers for any purchased item and may include the downstream portion of the supply chain. The *mapping* uses the concept of nodes to define the role of entities, and links represent flows and include the flow of materials, services, funds, and information.

- **Concept of "Preferred Customer"** refers to establishing a positive relationship with suppliers and vendors for advantages not readily available to other customers and yielding a competitive advantage in adversity. The relationship of customer with supplier is based on the positive behavior as in *pay on time, share relevant information, treat suppliers ethically,* and *empathize with supplier by "stepping into their shoes"* etc. The size of the contract or *size of the supplier* is of no consequence.

- **"DeCluster the Clusters"** relates to Michael Porters' referred connection between business or industry clusters and competitive advantage. Cluster represents *geographic concentration* of linked businesses that enjoy unusual competitive success in their field. Firms, unlike dispersed buyers and sellers acting collectively to promote trust, interdependence, coordination, innovation, and communication, organizations tend to take advantage of clusters for improving logistics costs, government incentives, labor availability, and easy availability of SC components, to name a few advantages. However, there are inherent risks attached to clusters as a single risk or threat can impact everybody, *crippling the service to the customer.* Organizations are de-risking from clusters by sourcing from suppliers from different regions, shifting production plants from *risk prone areas*, diversifying plant capacity in different regions/countries, reconsidering distribution and receipt points, and asking suppliers to de-risk from a single source, etc.

- **"Flexible Supply Chain"** refers to adaptable and responsive changes to the supply chain, especially with the change of risk and its impact severity. This flexibility adds choices for SC resiliency and adapts quickly to risk events, including change in demand and disruption in supply while maintaining customer service levels. The various types of flexibility could be listed as SC flexibility; flexibility of material, production, and delivery; volume and capacity flexibility; energy and workforce scheduling flexibility; energy flexibility with different energy sources and suppliers; and site flexibility, where production is shifted among locations and between suppliers.

Conclusion

In conclusion, it is fair to say that *"when being chased by a bear, you don't have to outrun the bear – you just have to overrun the other guy,"* meaning in business, we only must run a bit faster than our competitors to be successful. This is so true for all our domains in discussion, SCRM, CM, BCM, and RM. Risks and threats are a reality of our corporate environment, yet when risk events do occur or a crisis strikes, it is important for organizations to be fast, flexible, responsive, and prepared to face the situation with stoic effectiveness to come out successful in protecting the organization's reputation, customers, and stakeholder interest. In doing so, the management must understand the nuances of SCRM and its impact on preparedness for dealing with crisis, a situation requiring BC Plan invocation and mitigating the risk factors while understanding the common elements and leveraging the solution for universal benefit under the different management plans governing these four domains.

Key Take-Aways

- SCRM is synthesized with organization CM and BCM for its resilience.
- Supply chain vulnerabilities must be analyzed, and mitigation plans should be developed in "peace time."
- Use technology as an enabler to deal with new emerging risks and threats.

Chapter 11

Management Involvement in BCM Test and Exercise

Its Depth

At the end of the day, it is the management team of organizations that *holds the can*, should any untoward incident impact it. The managers need to re-assure themselves that the organization is resilient and will be able to withstand any crisis or emergency. It is for this reason that the managers and organization management should participate in business continuity management (BCM) tests and exercises to understand its preparedness levels, ensure that staff are aware of their specific role and responsibility during a crisis and emergency, and have knowledge of internal and external factors.

The expression *the proof of the pudding is in the eating* is used to emphasize that the real worth, success, or effectiveness of something can only be determined by putting it to the test – by trying it or using it. This holds very true in the context of the success of the business continuity program in any organization, where unless the initiative is tested, its purpose and its ability to meet the required objective cannot be relied upon.

This chapter specifically covers the importance of testing and exercising and why it is recommended that there should be adequate senior management involvement in this important exercise. We have observed that the business continuity program has a better chance of being effective when *driven from the top,* and accordingly, the personnel *take it seriously as the diktat is coming from senior management.* The senior managers should also be wary of these tests and exercises for them to happen on time, on a regular basis, and to meet their objective.

The organizations must have a coherent strategy for testing their business continuity and crisis readiness, including the type of test and its schedule. Untested plans can give an unrealistic degree of confidence and *push organizations in deeper trouble* in case they are unable to manage a crisis properly. The test must delve into the staff readiness, crucial logistics, supply chain risk, pandemic preparedness, technology prowess, and other support elements. It is equally important that the outcome of the test and

DOI: 10.4324/9781003304678-11

open issues of these tests are analyzed, and if found lacking, the same should be acted upon for its non-occurrence in the future. The BCM team should be careful not to *overdo* these tests and exercises, lest they get reduced to a *tick in the box initiative*.

The tests and exercise should create incremental confidence for all staff of the organization, and senior management should positively relate with respect to the effectiveness of the business continuity program. For this reason, the tests/exercise should be properly planned and conducted regularly as per schedule. Testing and exercising require technical resources, equipment, and facility resources to conduct a successful test and the related expertise to devise such a plan.

Senior management should ensure they get involved in all aspects of the tests and namely:

1 Formulation of a test plan covering testing of critical functions.
2 Test scenario planning, its success criterion, its protocol, etc.
3 Ensuring the test addresses the needs of operations as well as financial and administrative requirements.
4 The test/exercise plan should include the organization pain points and measures for a solution during a crisis.
5 Test objectives being in line with the overall organization strategy.
6 Thorough *"Pre-Planning"* with a realistic scenario and timely injects with due training of team members for their recovery roles.
7 Plan addressing the needs of all stakeholders and the *"buy-in"* of resources required for the test/exercise.
8 Appointment of observers, their role and responsibility.
9 Validation of the true length of recovery time and ability to achieve the pre-defined RTO (recovery time objective).
10 Format of Test Report, detailing open issues with clarity of owners and target closure date, etc.

It will be observed that the above factors not only cover the aspect of the test/exercise considering end-to-end requirements of running critical operations during a crisis, but these also cover comprehensively the coordination of the internal and external parties for support during a crisis. The internal parties refer to the different departments within the enterprise, and external refers to the vendor, suppliers, and service providers. It is crucial for the organization that all these different *players* play their roles effectively during a crisis in a timely manner and in coordination with the *need of the crisis hour*.

Apart from the benefit of the above-listed factors, the involvement of senior management in tests and exercises also has numerous other advantages for different stakeholders, namely its employees, its senior managers, its customers, its service providers, etc. The important ones are listed here:

1 Senior management involvement enhances the effectiveness and impact of the initiative as the same is being *driven top down*.
2 Senior management, based on the conduct of the test/exercise, is aware of any specific requirement and need for adhering to any specific or special requirement to be complied with by the organization, e.g., requirement as specified by the Regulator.
3 Testing reveals missing steps.
4 Senior management with due participation in the test is better placed to anticipate and have the knowledge during any crisis situation for a timely and appropriate decision before the escalation of the situation.
5 Preparation of personnel, process, and equipment to deal with #3 above.
6 Proactively arrange for finances and partners for dealing with a crisis and ensuring continuity of critical operations.
7 With the involvement of senior management, there is better scope for an exercise getting 100% support and buy-in of both internal and external participants.
8 Senior management can ensure inclusion of important aspect of any future requirement while considering organizational growth and expansion plans.
9 The management can incorporate any specific requirements that get included in the test and exercise while incorporating the market's best practices, especially those adopted by other industry participants.
10 For the purpose of adopting new technology and upgraded solutions for aiding organization resilience, management can include a part of the test/exercise using the new technology in the *test environment*.

Conclusion

From all the points and benefits mentioned above, it can be inferred that the crisis and disruption may be on account of different events, yet it is relevant to note *how quick was the flow of data and details of the incident to senior management for them to take the right decision without any delay*.

It is for this reason that these tests validate the functionality of the plans and the organization's ability to deal with the crisis without any *major downside*. Senior management should therefore always be willing to participate in the tests and exercises on a regular basis.

Key Take-Aways

- The organization must have clearly documented BCM test and exercise plans, and its management must ensure conduct of the test/exercise as per calendar.
- Management must contribute their bit in planning, scheduling, and participation in testing of plans.
- Management, guided by the financial numbers (definite impact of downtime/outage), must ensure the test covers mitigating the risks and threats.

Epilogue

Managements and Boards of organizations across the globe are fraught with multiple priorities that demand their attention and the need for considered and timely decisions. The senior leaders must balance their time and energy for seeking and realizing opportunities that come their way and dealing with accompanying risks and threats that could shake the very edifice of the organization if there is negligence in taking and initiating the right action.

These diversions for the management may relate to issues of a diverse nature, for example, financial and economic focus, investment decisions pertaining to returns, technology, competition, market share, product innovation, etc. The common factor among these is that all of them have a significant impact on the organization's future and can make or break things for the future existence of the organization.

The author has covered the diverse aspects for company's Board of Directors, CEOs, CXOs, CTOs, and Senior Management on how to specifically focus on key considerations to address the downside during a crisis, emergency, and disaster situation that may threaten an organization's existence in the future. The author has covered these in different chapters that address an issue in its entirety as he follows the approach of a "Cradle to Grave" concept while considering the 360 degrees view whilst considering the plusses and minuses for comprehensive solutioning. In doing so, he has also listed the key take-aways that can be readily used by readers and practitioners as tested and proven methods that have added to the resilience of the organizations and have bestowed confidence in personnel for being crisis ready.

The book addresses the vital aspect of risks and threats facing any organization and offers solutions for practicing basic business continuity even though it may be facing the rough weather of being in the red in terms of ROI and profitability. In doing so the author suggests ways and means to recognize and address internal and external threats that can prove fatal if these contingencies materialize.

The book offers excellent reference points for leaders and senior managers while understanding the relevance and relationship among crisis and risk management, its relation to continuity of critical operations, and the vital role played by technology as a *"key enabler"* for recovery of the operations within a reasonable period of time, covered in detail in the chapter on technology resilience.

The chapter on capital consideration covers the critical points of how much to invest, when to invest, and what to consider when the organization is embarking on its initiative of business continuity journey. There are important pointers to the specific requirements for type of personnel, training needs, and steps for effective BCM implementation under the aegis of Board/top management. These pointers can be important lessons for recovery during a crisis/ emergency that protects an organization's reputation and corporate integrity while also meeting the interests and needs of its important stakeholders.

The book offers some of the best practices in business continuity implementation for any organization in any industry. There is a reference to a universal approach that will help organization leaders to plan, execute, and implement the business continuity program effectively while adopting an entity-wide approach for its reinforcement as a corporate program for the benefit of each stakeholder of the organization. There is good reference of *imperative foundation factors* coupled with those relating to costs and resources that guide the bottom-line financial aspect and top line qualitative factors that add to the company's resilience.

Apart from covering the best practices, a chapter has been devoted to BCM in hard times. Whether the company is in the green or the red, it must adopt the basic principle of having a *Plan B* for a crisis and emergency, and in doing so, it must make the minimum investment in basic BCM, even if it is at a cost of a productive option. This is more relevant if, God forbid, bad times befall the organization or the ROI/profitability takes a knock due to market developments exacerbated by risks of cyber threats, global economic downturn, wars, political upheavals, etc. Other than these, at times the fast decision and action by competitors, inefficient operational practices and disjointed organization culture, and failed plans and strategies also contribute to companies hitting rough weather and pushing the organization into obsolescence. The author lists over 20 factors that befall in difficult times and over 15 factors that can aid in the success of a BCM team in any organization.

The author, through his advice for *automating BCM*, covers the vital factors that leaders and senior managers must understand in terms of the maturity of the organization and its people for *going in for a BCM tool* and provides comprehensive guidance regarding the tool's cost, age, suitability to the organization's needs and the role of the tool provider, and important factors in the case of tool procurement from a re-seller. There is adequate detailing of important considerations on components of tool cost, its training requirements, and practices that will yield the best optimum benefits from deployment of the BCM tool.

The readers can benefit from the vast experience of the author covering diverse industries, different geographies, and implementation and consulting to organizations in the private and public sector. The chapter on BCM implementation in O&G and Supply Chain Resiliency offers some key solutions and suggestions. These relate to skills and experience of personnel, relevance of training/retraining, the importance of awareness of the business continuity program, its structure and governance, and the importance of sourcing and deploying the right personnel for success in maintaining the organization resilience, as *business continuity implementation is not a choice but as imperative* for the organization in today's dynamic and risk- and threat-infested corporate environment.

The book will serve as a good reference guide for identifying the HR aspect of hiring the right person with the education, experience, and skills in line with the competency framework developed by UK's The Business Continuity Institute that specifies the standards required for effective performance by a business continuity practitioner. The reader will get insight into resource planning, deployment, and development of organization resilience capability. Leaders and senior managers can benefit from the suggestions by the author that elaborate on the challenge in business continuity and how these can be transformed for effective resilience at the enterprise level. This has also contributed to the transformation from cost-oriented convention to reward-related, management-focused initiative.

The author's extensive experience in practical implementation and consulting in these domains aids his guidance and advice to Boards, CEOs, and COOs with respect to factors they tend to miss for effective implementation of a business continuity program, and such are the factors that hinder success of the business continuity program. The inputs of the chapter where leadership falters in BCM implementation highlights the lacunae due to misconception about their *crisis readiness* and the fact of the organization being a *Tiger turning out to be a Paper Tiger*.

A chapter has been dedicated to the relevance and importance of management's focus and participation in the testing and exercise of BCPs. A successful testing would yield enterprise-wide confidence in its ability to deal with a crisis or emergency. The chapter elaborates on the advantages due to role clarity during crisis.

BCM managers and practitioners will gain a great deal from studying this book. Even seasoned BCM professionals would gain greatly from reviewing the many structured and valuable facts and information within this book. Written mainly from a practitioner's perspective, much of the information is practical and applicable to developing and implementing effective BCM systems.

Index

Printed in the United States
by Baker & Taylor Publisher Services